The 50

Best Cheesecakes

in the World

The 50

Best Cheesecakes

in the World

The Recipes That Won the Nationwide
"Love That Cheesecake" Contest

• • •

Larry and Honey Zisman

ST. MARTIN'S PRESS ✦ NEW YORK

Library of Congress Cataloging-in-Publication Data

    Zisman, Larry.
      The 50 best cheesecakes in the world / Larry and Honey Zisman.
        p. cm.
      ISBN 0-312-09239-3
      1. Cheesecake (Cookery) I. Zisman, Honey. II. Title.
    III. Title: Fifty best cheesecakes in the world.
    TX773.Z58 1993
    641.8'53—dc20   93-899
                                            CIP

20 19 18 17 16 15 14 13 12 11

Special thanks, recognition,
and appreciation for many books together
to:

Meg Ruley,
our marvelous agent at the Jane Rotrosen Agency

Barbara Anderson,
our magnificent editor at St. Martin's Press

Dedicated to
Anne Rose Weinmann Kligerman,
whose cheesecake started it all

· ANNE ROSE'S CHEESECAKE ·

CRUST

½ cup butter, melted
1¼ cups graham cracker crumbs
1 tablespoon flour

2 tablespoons sugar
1 teaspoon cinnamon

FILLING

1¼ pounds dry cottage cheese or
    farmer cheese
4 ounces cream cheese
1 cup sugar
1 heaping tablespoon cornstarch
2 eggs

juice of half a lemon
6 tablespoons cream
6 tablespoons milk
1 teaspoon vanilla
cinnamon

1. To make crust, mix together butter, graham cracker crumbs, flour, sugar, and cinnamon.

2. Pat into the bottom and up the sides of a 9½-inch glass pie pan. Set aside.

3. Preheat oven to 400° F.

4. To make filling, mix together in an electric mixer at medium speed cottage cheese or farmer cheese and cream cheese until smooth.

5. Add sugar, cornstarch, eggs, lemon juice, cream, milk, and vanilla.

6. Pour filling into crust, sprinkle cinnamon over top, and bake for 20 to 25 minutes. Cheesecake will not be set in middle.

7. Remove from oven and let cool on a wire rack for 1 to 2 hours. Chill for 4 to 6 hours before serving.

Yield: One 9½-inch cheesecake

If you just want to smile,
say, "CHEESE,"
but when you want to smile
and be really happy,
say, "CHEESECAKE."

Contents

Cheesecake—
Glorious Cheesecake

We all like cheesecake.

No, that's not right. We more than like cheesecake.

We love cheesecake.

In fact, we are positively passionate about cheesecake.

Think about the following:

- a truck-stop diner in New Jersey
- a dude ranch in Colorado
- a movie industry meeting place in California
- a trendy new bistro in Washington, D.C.
- a landmark delicatessen in New York
- a seafood place in Maine
- a luxury hotel in Florida
- a barbecue-pit restaurant in Texas
- a steak house in Nebraska
- a beach resort in North Carolina

What do all of these places have in common besides serving good food to happy diners?

Easy!

No matter which part of the country, no matter what kind of food is served, and no matter what the prices are on the menu, just about everywhere you eat out you can get cheesecake for dessert!

And if you are eating at home, just about everyone has a cherished family cheesecake recipe passed down from generation to generation that, as every family member will swear, makes "the best cheesecake you ever tasted."

Why this fascination with cheesecake?

It can't be because we eat so much cheese, although, on average, each American eats about 24 pounds of cheese a year.

If we ate cheesecake merely because we liked cheese, wouldn't there be a "ham-and-cheese" cheesecake, a "cheeseburger" cheesecake, or a "grilled cheese" cheesecake?

But, no, there isn't.

So the reasons we love cheesecake must be because it is delicious, it is satisfying, it is comforting, it comes in a great variety of flavors, and it appeals to almost everyone.

Could you ask for anything more?

Of course you could!

And what you could ask for would be the best of this wonderful dessert . . . and what you would get would be the 50 winners in the "LOVE THAT CHEESECAKE" contest.

Here are the winning recipes that will give you, your friends, your family, and everyone else who knows and enjoys the best in cheesecakes 50 more reasons why cheesecake is . . . and will continue to be . . . their favorite dessert.

And for even greater enjoyment of this favorite dessert, there is a fabulous addition to the 50 winning "LOVE THAT CHEESECAKE" recipes.

Wonderful cheesecake recipes have also been gathered from some of the best-known and most prestigious restaurants and hotels in the land . . . and on the sea. These "Cheesecakes from Special Places" are all together in the last chapter, a most fitting finale to this cheesecake treasury.

So enjoy all 50 . . . and more . . . recipes, discovering new passions on your dessert plate.

Helpful Hints for Making the Perfect Cheesecake

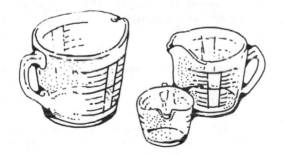

Contrary to what many inexperienced—and even some well-seasoned—home bakers believe, making a tasty, perfectly textured cheesecake does not have to be a difficult and daunting adventure.

Making a successful cheesecake should not be intimidating.

Millions of satisfied home bakers say, "Yes, I made that wonderful, delicious cheesecake myself."

You will go a long way toward demystifying cheesecake baking and become a worthy member of this happy group by following a few simple guidelines.

INGREDIENTS AND SUBSTITUTIONS

- Be sure to read your recipe through completely before starting to bake. That way you'll know just what ingredients and utensils to have on hand and how much time to allow for baking, cooling, and chilling your cheesecake.
- Some home bakers have a very good procedure to make sure they do not leave anything out of the recipe. Place all the ingredients in the appropriate order on the countertop before you start, and as you measure and add each ingredient remove the package or the measuring container for that ingredient. Then you will know that if an ingredient is gone, it was included.
- Whenever possible, use fresh ingredients instead of prepackaged. There is definitely a real difference when you use fresh squeezed lemon juice instead of bottled. Freshly scraped lime zest is superior to dried. "Fresh" perks up everything you make, not just cheesecakes.
- You can get away with less expensive, generic brands of chocolate or cream cheese or other ingredients, but there is a difference in taste. But

the difference matters more regarding who is going to eat your cheesecake than in your own sensibilities in making it.

If you are making a cheesecake for a bunch of teenagers who just vacuum up any food left unattended, you can use the lesser goods. But if you are hosting the monthly meeting of the local gourmet society or a gathering of food editors, go with the genuine, traditional ingredients and the more expensive brands that you have tried and know to be not just more expensive in price, but also superior in quality.

- Open the packages of cream cheese before letting it soften, since it will be much easier to scrape the cheese off the foil wrapper. And it is helpful to cut up the cream cheese into small pieces for easier mixing. It is better to have the cream cheese completely smooth before adding the other ingredients for the filling.
- Allow all the ingredients that were refrigerated to come to room temperature before you start making the cheesecake. This will give you a smoother and creamier cheesecake.
- Frequently scrape down the sides and bottom of the mixing bowl and the mixer blades to ensure a complete and even blending of all the ingredients.
- Yes, you can substitute and, yes, you can do it in many different ways. If a recipe calls for chopped pecans and you can't stand pecans but love hazelnuts, go right ahead and use hazelnuts . . . or walnuts or peanuts or whatever kind of nut you like. Fresh fruit can usually be replaced with well-drained canned fruit. Decaffeinated coffee can be used instead of regular.
- As a general rule, any liquid can be used in place of another one in the same amounts. Just keep in mind the changes in flavors. . . . Almond

flavoring instead of vanilla? Why not? . . . Orange liqueur instead of raspberry? Of course!

PREVENTING CRACKS IN YOUR CHEESECAKE

Sometimes cracks will appear on the top of your cheesecake as it is baking or after it comes out of the oven and it is cooling. This cracking happens because the cake dried out due to a too-high oven temperature during baking or was left in the oven too long. Small cracks that show up during baking sometimes will disappear afterward as the cake cools.

However, cheesecakes that show no cracks during baking could develop cracks after they come out of the oven if the cake is exposed to drafts or allowed to cool too rapidly by chilling it in the refrigerator before it is completely cooled.

Since many bakers don't like their cheesecakes to "crack up," there are, fortunately, several ways to prevent—or at least minimize—the cracking.

- Before baking, be sure to grease adequately the sides of the springform pan so the cheesecake will not stick when cooling as the cake shrinks.
- For you meticulous bakers who go the extra step, instead of casually greasing the pan before putting the crust in, you might consider chilling the pan thoroughly and then brushing the sides and bottom with melted butter. This method causes the butter to harden on the pan as it is greased and prevents the butter from dripping. Also, you get a more even coating on the inside of the pan and you are able to see if you have covered every spot with butter.
- Place a pan of hot water on a low rack in the oven below the cheesecake.

The steam that comes from the pan of water will provide moisture to the cheesecake as it is baking. The water level in the pan should be checked about halfway through the baking time and refilled as necessary.

Another method is to bake the cheesecake with the springform pan placed directly into a large roasting pan half-filled with water. The sides and bottom of the springform pan should be wrapped tightly with foil to prevent any water from seeping in. Again, the water level in the roasting pan should be checked about halfway through the baking time and refilled as necessary.

- Wrap the springform pan in foil even when it is not placed into a larger pan filled with water to prevent any of the batter from leaking out. Or if you don't want to bother wrapping the pan, it is a good idea to place the springform pan in the oven on a cookie tin with a lip or a rim to catch any leaking batter.

- To ensure even heat while baking, place your cheesecake on a middle rack in the oven evenly centered from the sides and the front and the back.

- Besides overcooking your cheesecake by leaving it in the oven too long, you can overcook a cheesecake by setting the oven temperature too high. And the temperature can be too high even if the recipe calls for 350° F and you set your oven for 350° F. Not all ovens maintain the exact temperature that is set. It is a good idea to keep an oven thermometer inside and check the exact temperature of your oven against the setting of the temperature control and adjust accordingly. You can buy an oven thermometer at any cookware or hardware store . . . and they are not expensive.

- Although you are sure to be excited about your cheesecake as it is baking and you really want to see what's going on in the oven, resist the temptation to open the door and peek inside at least until half the required baking time has passed. This way the baking temperature will remain more constant, and you'll get a better cheesecake if it is not disturbed during the first half of the baking.
- Since overcooking can cause cracks, obviously avoid overcooking your cheesecakes. It is easy to test a regular cake to see if it is done baking. You just stick a toothpick in it, and when it comes out clean the cake is done. But when it comes to testing a cheesecake, the toothpick will always come out with cheesecake on it even if you bake it for an extra hour or two.

  So how do you tell when it is done?

  First of all, the top of the cheesecake should have changed from the shiny uncooked or undercooked cake to a dull surface. Second, the center of the cheesecake should move only slightly when the pan is gently tapped. When the recipe says the cheesecake is done when the cheesecake is "set," that means the center no longer moves when shaken. An "almost set" cheesecake is one where a two- to three-inch circle in the middle wiggles when it is shaken.

  One warning, though. While waiting for your cheesecake to be "set" or "almost set," keep an eye on the edge of the crust to make sure that it is not starting to burn. The crust should not get any more done than just golden brown, regardless of how set the filling is. Keep in mind that cheesecakes will harden somewhat after the baking is finished.
- Unless the recipe says otherwise, when the cheesecake is done baking

let it cool in the oven with the heat off and the door ajar for about an hour so it can cool slowly and be protected from any drafts.

- Running a thin knife around the inside edge of the springform pan to separate the cake from the pan as the cheesecake is cooling will give even more assurance against cracking. Separating the cake from the pan during the cooling prevents the sides of the cake from being pulled down by the pan as they cool at different rates.
- Although there are a lot of things that can cause you to panic, having your cheesecake rise up during baking and sink down during cooling should not be one of them. Such movement by your cheesecake is normal.

If, despite all your precautions and your being a good person and calling your mother every night, cracks do appear, do not get upset and consider yourself a failure as a human being . . . or not a decent and worthy person. Cheesecake cracks can happen even to saintly people and Nobel Prize winners.

What, then, should you do about cracks, besides calling them "character lines" and saying that they make your cheesecake a more interesting dessert? This question assumes, of course, that you are too mortified and embarrassed to serve a cracked cheesecake.

- Just cover the cracks up with any one or two of a multitude of available toppings, such as fruit glazes, fresh fruit, whipped cream, chocolate shavings, prepared fruit pie fillings, chocolate sauce, crushed cookies and candies, coconut flakes, mint leaves, and granola. The only limit is your imagination and personal tastes.

Your family, friends, and guests will remark favorably on your creativity and culinary expertise in making such tasty additions.

MASTERING THE ART OF THE SPRINGFORM PAN

- The best way to remove the bottom metal plate of a springform pan after you have finished making the cheesecake is not to remove it at all. Just leave the baked cheesecake right on the pan bottom when you serve it. The bottom of the pan cannot be seen, since it is completely covered by the cheesecake.

  Be a little careful putting the cheesecake on a serving dish, since the pan bottom can be slippery and the cheesecake could easily slide right off the serving plate and onto the floor. To save yourself from this potential mess and embarrassment, place one of those thin rubber grips you use to open stuck jar lids on the serving plate and then put the cheesecake on top of the rubber grip.

- If you don't want to tie up the pan bottom until the cheesecake is all gone, you could make your own pan bottom out of cardboard and foil. Cut out a nine-inch circle (or whatever size your springform pan is) from a piece of cardboard and then completely and tightly wrap the circle in foil. Voilà! You have a springform pan bottom that is entirely disposable.

  Or you could go to a gourmet, cookware, or handsomely stocked hardware store and buy some precut cardboard pizza pie disks. No gourmet or hardware shop around? Check out your neighborhood pizza shop and grovel and beg until they give you several pie disks . . . and, while you are there, order a good pepperoni and mushroom pizza to enjoy before eating the cheesecake.

- If you have borrowed someone else's springform pan, or if you have to use the same pan again right away, or if you want to give your home-baked cheesecake as a gift (what a thoughtful and appreciated idea, but good luck on getting your pan bottom back), there is a way to remove your cheesecake from the bottom of the pan.

Are you ready?

Chill the cheesecake still in the springform pan in the refrigerator for several hours, ensuring that it is completely cooled. Remove the sides of the pan and then, using a *really big* spatula, preferably one as long as or longer than the cheesecake is wide, *carefully* slide the spatula between the cheesecake and the bottom of the pan and *very carefully* ease the cake off the pan bottom onto a serving plate.

- What do you do when the recipe calls for a different-sized springform pan than what you have? While it is always best—perhaps even absolutely essential—to use the exact size indicated, you might be able to use another pan after some trial and error. For example, if the recipe calls for a 9-inch springform pan and all you have is a ten-inch pan, the cheesecake will not be as high as usual and will probably require less cooking time. On the other hand, if all you have is an eight-inch pan for the nine-inch pan recipe, you will have a little batter left over and the cooking time might vary from what is stated.

The real solution to this kind of situation is experimentation and then applying your newly learned baking knowledge.

SERVING AND STORING YOUR CHAMPION CHEESECAKE

- When serving your cheesecake, unless it is specifically stated otherwise in the recipe, the best cheesecake flavor comes out when it is served at room temperature or just slightly chilled. Remove the cheesecake from the refrigerator about thirty minutes to one hour before serving.

- Cutting a cheesecake into serving pieces requires a little more care than cutting a regular layer cake, but do not despair. You can expertly slice a cheesecake without turning it into cheesecake crumbs. All you have to do is follow some easy suggestions.

- It is best to use a good, sharp knife—not a cake server—for the actual cutting. You may lift up and serve each slice with a cake server, but do not do the actual cutting with the server.

- Wet the knife with hot water, the hotter the better, and *wet the knife again before each cut*. If you are cutting the cheesecake at the table, have close by a deep container of very hot water and dip the knife into the water after each slice. It is even better if you cut the cake in the kitchen, so you can run the knife under very hot water between slices.

- For those occasions when you are unable to have hot water available for wetting the knife between slices, thoroughly wipe off the knife in between each cutting.

  If you would rather not use a knife and want to give your guests something to talk about, cut your cheesecake with dental floss, heavy button thread, or nylon fishing line. Hold the string very tightly with both hands and slowly and carefully run the string down through the cake. Pull the string out once you get to the bottom rather than trying to pull it back up through the cut.

  Most guests think they will not see dental floss until they return home, but they will be surprised to see it on your table.

- If for some strange reason you don't want to eat your cheesecake right away or, even stranger, there is some left over, you can freeze it. Make sure the cheesecake is completely cooled and the pan sides are removed. First wrap the cake completely airtight with plastic wrap and then cover completely with heavy-duty foil.

- Soon after freezing your cheesecake you will realize that you made a dreadful mistake and you really want to eat it as soon as possible . . . not days, weeks, or months in the future. However, defrosting a cheesecake must be done slowly and properly or it will not come out right.

   Place the frozen cheesecake, still completely wrapped, in the refrigerator, not on a counter- or tabletop, and let it sit undisturbed for about twelve hours. Then unwrap the cheesecake and leave it in the refrigerator until it is completely defrosted. Remove it from the refrigerator about thirty minutes to an hour before serving.

   Wasn't it worth waiting for to do it right?

One last thought.

Cheesecakes are usually enjoyed just for themselves rather than in connection with special events like other cakes are.

Is that right?

Is that necessary?

Why not have a birthday or anniversary cheesecake complete with candles? How about a national holiday cheesecake decorated in patriotic colors and with several sparklers shooting off? And think about a Christmas cheesecake with holly leaves or a Valentine's Day treat decorated with red cinnamon hearts arranged on top.

They'll love you for it!

Eight-Inch
Cheesecakes

· KEY LIME CHEESECAKE ·

Nanc Piper
Miami, Florida

Think of the most romantic images of the Florida Keys and you will find them all in this ultimate creamy, tangy, lime-flavored delight.

CRUST

1½ cups graham cracker crumbs   2 tablespoons sugar
2 tablespoons margarine

FILLING

2 extra-large eggs, separated   ¼ cup key lime juice
2 tablespoons sugar   1 cup sugar
1 pound cream cheese

1. Preheat oven to 350° F.
2. To make crust, mix together graham crackers, margarine, and sugar.
3. Press into the bottom and up the sides of an 8-inch cake pan, an 8-inch pie pan, or an 8-inch springform pan.
4. Bake for 5 minutes, remove from oven, and set aside.
5. To make filling, beat egg whites until stiff with an electric mixer set on medium speed.

6. Add 2 tablespoons sugar and beat about 2 minutes, until sugar is absorbed. Set aside.

7. Beat together cream cheese and egg yolks.

8. Add key lime juice and 1 cup sugar, beating about 2 to 3 minutes, until smooth.

9. Fold in beaten egg whites. Mix by hand until smooth.

10. Pour batter into crust and bake for 40 to 45 minutes, until lightly brown. Do not open oven door for the first 35 minutes of baking.

11. Remove from oven and let cool on a wire rack for 1 to 2 hours. Refrigerate for about 4 hours before serving.

Yield: One 8-inch cheesecake

• HAZELNUT HEAVEN •

Thelma Silberman
Hallandale, Florida

Some people call them hazelnuts, some people call them filberts, but everyone will call this creamy cheesecake "delicious."

1 cup hazelnuts
2 pounds cream cheese, softened
1¾ cups sugar
4 eggs

½ teaspoon fresh lemon zest
⅓ cup graham cracker crumbs
whole hazelnuts

1. Preheat oven to 350° F.
2. Spread 1 cup hazelnuts in a shallow pan and bake for 3 to 5 minutes, stirring occasionally, until lightly browned.
3. Remove from oven, let cool slightly, and then rub with fingers to remove skins.
4. Grind hazelnuts in a blender. A slightly uneven texture is acceptable. Set aside.
5. With an electric mixer set on medium speed, beat cream cheese until very smooth, scraping sides of bowl often.
6. Beat in sugar until well blended.
7. Add eggs, one at a time, beating just to blend after each addition.
8. Stir in lemon zest and ground hazelnuts.
9. Pour batter into a buttered 8-inch springform pan. Place springform pan into a large roasting pan filled with 1½ inches of water.

10. Bake for 1½ hours. Check water level halfway through baking, adding more water if necessary.

11. Remove from oven and let cool 2 to 3 hours on a wire rack.

12. Invert cheesecake on a flat plate, remove from pan, and pat sides and bottom with graham cracker crumbs.

13. Quickly turn cheesecake right side up onto serving plate. Decorate with whole hazelnuts. Refrigerate for 5 to 6 hours.

Yield: One 8-inch cheesecake

• CHOCOLATE MALT CHEESECAKE •

Vi Gorham
Elk Grove Village, Illinois

You have certainly enjoyed creamy chocolate malted milk shakes. Now you are ready to enjoy this creamy chocolate malted cheesecake.

CRUST

1½ cups graham cracker crumbs
1 tablespoon sugar

6 tablespoons butter, melted

FILLING

1½ pounds cream cheese, softened
⅓ cup sugar
⅔ cup chocolate malted milk
    powder

¼ cup milk
1 teaspoon vanilla
3 eggs

GARNISH

10 to 12 malted milk balls,
    coarsely crushed

10 to 12 malted milk balls, cut in
    half

1. Preheat oven to 400° F.
2. To make crust, combine graham cracker crumbs, sugar, and butter, mixing together well.
3. Press evenly into the bottom of a greased 8-inch springform pan.
4. Bake for 5 minutes. Remove from oven and set aside to cool.
5. Reduce oven temperature to 325° F.
6. To make filling, with an electric mixer set on medium speed beat cream cheese and sugar until light and fluffy.
7. Stir malted milk powder into milk until dissolved, and pour into cream cheese mixture.
8. Add vanilla and beat at medium speed for 2 minutes.
9. Add eggs, one at a time, beating well after each addition.
10. Pour filling into crust and bake at 325° F. for 1 hour.
11. Turn off oven, open oven door slightly, and let cheesecake sit in the oven for another 15 minutes.
12. Remove from oven and let cool on a wire rack for 1 hour. Run a knife around sides of cheesecake to loosen. Remove rim of pan.
13. Garnish by firmly but gently pressing crushed malted milk balls into sides of cheesecake. Decorate top of cake with malted milk ball halves, cut side down.
14. Loosely cover cheesecake with foil and refrigerate for at least 3 hours.

Yield: One 8-inch cheesecake

• TERRI'S PEACHY KEEN CHEESECAKE •

Terri Louise Ross
Santa Ana, California

You might not find "peachy keen" in the dictionary, but with this cheesecake it means "marvelous," with a shiny glazed peach top, a chocolate-almond cheese filling, and an almond cookie crust.

CRUST

1½ cups almond cookie crumbs
1 tablespoon sugar

1 tablespoon cinnamon
2 tablespoons butter or margarine, melted

FILLING

1 pound cream cheese, softened
1 cup sugar
¼ cup cocoa powder
3 eggs

½ teaspoon almond extract
1 cup sour cream
¼ cup peach schnapps

GLAZE

⅓ cup sugar
2 tablespoons cornstarch
¾ cup peach nectar

¼ cup peach schnapps
3 fresh peaches, peeled and sliced

GARNISH

whipped cream

1. To make crust, combine cookie crumbs, sugar, cinnamon, and butter or margarine, mixing together well.

2. Press into the bottom and 1½ inches up the sides of an 8-inch springform pan. Chill.

3. Preheat oven to 350° F.

4. To make filling, with an electric mixer set on medium speed beat cream cheese, sugar, and cocoa powder.

5. Add eggs, almond extract, and sour cream, beating until smooth.

6. Stir in schnapps.

7. Pour filling into crust and bake for 40 to 50 minutes.

8. Remove from oven and let cool on a wire rack for 1 to 2 hours.

9. To make glaze, combine sugar, cornstarch, and peach nectar in a saucepan and cook over medium heat, stirring constantly, until mixture boils. Simmer for 1 minute.

10. Remove from heat and add schnapps. Let cool to lukewarm.

11. Spoon ¼ of glaze over top of cooled cheesecake. Arrange peach slices in a semi-circle on top of glaze. Spoon remaining glaze over peach slices.

12. Chill until glaze is firm—about 1 to 2 hours—and then remove rim of pan.

13. Garnish with whipped cream.

Yield: One 8-inch cheesecake

⋅ CITRUS CLOUD ⋅

Mary Bennett Zelensky
Burlington, New Jersey

You will be floating on air when you eat this light cheesecake with a distinctive, refreshing orange-lemony flavor.

CRUST

2 cups flour
1/4 cup sugar
finely grated zest of 1/2 lemon

2/3 cup butter, chopped into small
   pieces the size of peas
1 egg, beaten

FILLING

1 1/2 pounds cream cheese, softened
1 cup sour cream
2/3 cup sugar
2 tablespoons flour
4 egg yolks

4 egg whites, beaten until frothy
finely grated zest and juice of
   1 orange
finely grated zest and juice of 1
   lemon
1/2 teaspoon vanilla

GARNISH

confectioners' sugar   *mandarin orange slices, well
                                            drained*

1. To make crust, place flour into a large bowl and use hands to fluff up flour and press out any small lumps.

2. Add sugar and lemon zest, mixing well.

3. Add butter pieces and egg and work in with hands to form a smooth dough. Wrap in silver foil and refrigerate for at least 30 minutes.

4. To make filling, with an electric mixer set on medium speed beat together cream cheese, sour cream, sugar, flour, and egg yolks.

5. Fold in egg whites.

6. Stir in orange zest, orange juice, lemon zest, lemon juice, and vanilla. Mix until smooth. Set aside.

7. Preheat oven to 475° F.

8. Remove crust from refrigerator and roll out on a lightly floured surface to a thickness of ¼ inch.

9. Line a greased 8-inch springform pan with crust. Spoon filling into crust.

10. Bake for 15 minutes at 475° F.

11. Decrease oven temperature to 275° F. and bake for 50 minutes more.

12. Remove from oven and let cool on a wire rack for 1 to 2 hours.

13. Garnish cooled cheesecake with a dusting of confectioners' sugar and mandarin orange slices.

14. Chill for 4 to 6 hours.

Yield: One 8-inch cheesecake

• RHUBARB TART •

Jacqueline Davis
Bangor, Maine

A tangy, square cheesecake with rhubarb and a melt-in-your-mouth crust that pushes outward to new frontiers in cheesecake.

CRUST

½ cup butter or margarine,
    softened
1 tablespoon sugar

1 tablespoon candied orange peel
1 cup flour

FILLING

RHUBARB LAYER
½ cup sugar
¼ cup flour

1 pound rhubarb, cut into small
    pieces

CREAM CHEESE LAYER
8 ounces cream cheese, softened
½ cup sugar

1 egg

TOPPING

½ cup sour cream
1 tablespoon sugar

1 tablespoon candied orange peel

1. To make crust, combine butter or margarine, sugar, and orange peel.
2. Add flour, mixing until a dough forms.
3. Press evenly into the bottom and up the sides of a well-greased 8-inch or 9-inch square pan. Set aside.
4. Preheat oven to 450° F.
5. To make rhubarb layer, combine sugar, flour, and rhubarb.
6. Place evenly in crust and bake for 10 minutes.
7. Remove pan from oven and decrease oven temperature to 350° F.
8. To make cream cheese layer, with an electric mixer set on medium speed combine cream cheese and sugar, beating until fluffy.
9. Add egg and continue beating until creamy.
10. Pour over rhubarb layer and bake for 30 to 35 minutes. Remove from oven.
11. To make topping, blend sour cream, sugar, and orange peel. Spread evenly over cheesecake.
12. Chill several hours or overnight before serving.

Yield: One 8- or 9-inch cheesecake

Nine-Inch and Nine-and-a-Half-Inch Cheesecakes

◆ MARZIPAN-RASPBERRY CHEESECAKE ◆

Diane Mary Polansky Ward
Ankeny, Iowa

This cheesecake not only has the allure of almond and chocolate, but also makes a sparkling presentation covered with raspberry sauce and fresh raspberries.

CRUST

1½ cups finely crushed chocolate cream sandwich cookies

3 tablespoons butter or margarine, melted

FILLING

1½ pounds cream cheese, softened
8 ounces almond paste, crumbled
1 cup sugar

4 eggs
1 cup sour cream

TOPPING

12 ounces fresh raspberries
½ cup sugar

1 teaspoon fresh lemon juice

GARNISH

fresh whole raspberries

1. To make crust, combine cookie crumbs and butter or margarine.
2. Press into the bottom of a greased 9-inch springform pan. Set aside.
3. Preheat oven to 325° F.
4. To make filling, with an electric mixer set on medium speed beat together cream cheese and almond paste.
5. Beat in sugar until fluffy.
6. Add eggs and sour cream all at once, beating on low speed until just combined.
7. Pour filling into crust and bake for about 1 hour, until center is nearly set when gently shaken.
8. Remove from oven and let cool for 15 minutes. Loosen rim of pan and let cool for 30 minutes more. Remove rim and let cool completely, about 1 hour more.
9. Chill for 4 to 6 hours.
10. To make topping, with a food processor or blender blend raspberries until smooth, and then press through a sieve to remove seeds.
11. Combine pureed raspberries, sugar, and lemon juice in a saucepan and heat until sugar dissolves.
12. Remove from heat and let cool about 1 hour.
13. Chill thoroughly and then drizzle over top of chilled cheesecake.
14. Garnish with whole raspberries.

Yield: One 9-inch cheesecake

· WHITE CHRISTMAS CHEESECAKE ·

Irene E. Souza
Cupertino, California

Everyone, of course, dreams of a "White Christmas," and their dreams should include this very pretty, very delectable white chocolate joy.

CRUST

1½ cups vanilla wafer crumbs   ¼ cup margarine, melted

FILLING

1½ pounds cream cheese, softened   12 ounces white chocolate, melted
14 ounces sweetened condensed   2 teaspoons white crème de cacao
   milk
3 eggs

TOPPING

6 ounces white chocolate   ¼ cup heavy cream

GARNISH

⅔ cup heavy cream, whipped   angelica, cut into leaf-shaped
raspberries   pieces

1. To make crust, combine wafer crumbs and margarine and press into the bottom of a 9 inch springform pan. Set aside.

2. Preheat oven to 300° F.

3. To make filling, with an electric mixer on medium speed combine cream cheese and ¼ cup of the condensed milk and beat until fluffy.

4. Gradually beat in remaining condensed milk.

5. Add eggs, one at a time, beating well after each addition.

6. Blend in melted white chocolate and crème de cacao.

7. Pour filling into crust and bake for about 1 hour and 15 minutes, until set in middle.

8. Remove from oven. Let cool on a wire rack for 1 to 2 hours before removing rim of pan.

9. To make topping, melt chocolate and heavy cream in a heavy saucepan, mixing until smooth.

10. Spread topping evenly over cheesecake and chill until set, about 4 to 6 hours.

11. Garnish chilled cheesecake with whipped cream, using a pastry bag to pipe a border around the edge. Decorate with raspberries and angelica leaves.

Yield: One 9-inch cheesecake

• TROPICAL PASSION •

Patsey Reed
Irvine, California

This is not your usual cheesecake, and the abundance of tropical fruits and the toasted coconut crust will make you passionate for the out-of-the-ordinary.

CRUST

2 cups coconut flakes

¼ cup butter, melted

FILLING

¼ cup dried papaya pieces
¼ cup dried pineapple pieces
¼ cup dried apricot pieces
½ cup passion liqueur
1 pound cream cheese, softened

½ cup sugar
3 eggs
1 tablespoon cornstarch
freshly grated zest of 1 lime

GLAZE

1 cup pineapple preserves

2 tablespoons passion liqueur

tropical fruit slices (kiwi, papaya,
  mango, star fruit, etc.)

1. Preheat oven to 350° F.
2. To make crust, spread coconut on a cookie sheet and bake for about 6 minutes, until golden. Stir frequently to prevent burning.
3. Combine coconut and butter and press into the bottom of a buttered 9-inch springform pan.
4. Wrap bottom of pan with foil and place on a cookie sheet to catch any leaking butter during baking.
5. To make filling, soak papaya, pineapple, and apricot pieces in passion liqueur for at least 1 hour.
6. Preheat oven to 325° F.
7. With an electric mixer set on medium speed, beat cream cheese and sugar until fluffy.
8. Add eggs, one at a time, beating well after each addition.
9. Add cornstarch and lime zest.
10. Fold in undrained marinated dried fruits.
11. Pour filling into crust and bake for 40 minutes.
12. Turn off oven and release cheesecake from sides of pan with knife, but leave rim attached. Let cool to room temperature in oven with oven door slightly open.
13. To make glaze, cook pineapple preserves and passion liqueur over medium heat until mixture can be poured easily.

14. Press mixture through fine sieve, discarding solid pieces.

15. Spoon half of glaze evenly over top of cooled cheesecake. Garnish with slices of tropical fruits and then brush with remaining glaze.

16. Refrigerate for at least 4 hours. Serve cold.

Yield: One 9-inch cheesecake

It may not be politically correct these days to notice such things, but *Webster's Third New International Dictionary* gives as one definition of cheesecake "photography or photographs (as in advertisements or publicity) featuring the natural curves of shapely female legs, thighs, or trunk, usually scantily clothed—called also leg art."

More succinctly, *The American Heritage Dictionary*, 2d college ed., says cheesecake is "a photograph of a pretty girl scantily clothed."

"How," you ask, "did such pictures become known as cheesecake?"

There are various theories, but the one that has the greatest historic sanctification involves a news photographer named James Kane who worked for the *New York Journal* . . . and who really enjoyed cheesecake (the dessert, not necessarily the pictures).

One day in 1912 Kane was taking the stereotypical shipboard picture of a smiling actress posing along the rail on an incoming ocean liner. Just as he was taking the picture, a gust of wind lifted her skirt high enough so that the final picture showed, as the caustic-tongued journalist H. L. Mencken described it, "more of her person than either he or she suspected."

When Kane developed the picture in the darkroom, he was pleasantly surprised to see how his picture came out. Looking for the best way to express the highest praise and his uninhibited joy at the sight of the picture, he exclaimed, "That's real cheesecake!"

• JOHNNY'S CHOCOLATE TRUFFLE CHEESECAKE •

John S. Lurie, Jr.
St. Petersburg, Florida

Chocolate truffle candies are loved by everyone, and this cheesecake with its creamy chocolate filling and vanilla cookie crust will also have a special place in your heart.

CRUST

1½ cups vanilla cookie crumbs
¼ cup sugar

⅓ cup margarine, melted

FILLING

14 ounces sweetened condensed milk
¾ cup chocolate truffle liqueur, chilled
3-ounce package vanilla pudding

2 pounds cream cheese, softened
3 eggs
½ teaspoon chocolate extract

GARNISH

heavy cream, whipped

chocolate truffle candies, cut in half

1. Preheat oven to 325° F.
2. To make crust, mix together cookie crumbs, sugar, and margarine
3. Press into the bottom of a greased 9-inch springform pan.
4. Bake for 10 minutes. Remove from oven and set aside.
5. To make filling, in a saucepan combine condensed milk, chocolate truffle liqueur, and vanilla pudding.
6. Cook over medium heat, stirring until pudding is dissolved and mixture has thickened. Remove from heat and set aside.
7. With an electric mixer set on medium speed, beat cream cheese until fluffy.
8. Add eggs and chocolate extract, beating until smooth.
9. Blend in pudding mixture.
10. Pour filling into crust and bake for 15 minutes.
11. Reduce oven temperature to 225° F. and bake for 1 hour more.
12. Remove from oven and let cool on a wire rack for 1 to 2 hours.
13. Chill for 4 to 6 hours.
14. Garnish chilled cheesecake with whipped cream piped around the edge and chocolate truffle halves.

Yield: One 9-inch cheesecake

• PUMPKIN PARTY CHEESECAKE •

Kathleen Fadley
Columbus, Ohio

Here is the perfect dessert for Thanksgiving—or for any other time of the
year—when you want creamy pumpkin and crunchy nut all at the same time.

CRUST

¾ cup graham cracker crumbs
½ cup finely chopped pecans
¼ cup firmly packed light brown
   sugar

¼ cup sugar
¼ cup unsalted butter, melted and
   cooled

FILLING

1½ cups pumpkin (not pumpkin
   pie filling)
3 large eggs
1½ teaspoons cinnamon
½ teaspoon freshly grated nutmeg
½ teaspoon ground ginger
½ teaspoon salt
½ cup firmly packed light brown
   sugar

1½ pounds cream cheese, softened
½ cup sugar
2 tablespoons heavy cream
1 tablespoon cornstarch
1 teaspoon vanilla
1 tablespoon bourbon

2 cups sour cream   *1 tablespoon bourbon*
2 tablespoons sugar

GARNISH

16 pecan halves

1. To make crust, combine graham cracker crumbs, pecans, brown sugar, and sugar.
2. Stir in butter and press into the bottom and ½ inch up the sides of a 9-inch springform pan.
3. Chill for 1 hour.
4. Preheat oven to 350° F.
5. To make filling, whisk together pumpkin, eggs, cinnamon, nutmeg, ginger, salt, and brown sugar. Set aside.
6. Using an electric mixer set on medium speed, beat together cream cheese, sugar, cream, cornstarch, vanilla, and bourbon.
7. Beat in pumpkin mixture until smooth.
8. Pour filling into crust and bake for 50 to 55 minutes on the middle rack of the oven, until center is just set.
9. Remove from oven and let cool on a wire rack for 5 minutes.
10. To make topping, whisk together sour cream, sugar, and bourbon.
11. Spread evenly over top of cheesecake and then bake at 350 degrees for 5 minutes.

12. Remove from oven and let cheesecake cool in the pan on a wire rack for 1 to 2 hours.

13. Cover and chill overnight. Remove rim of pan.

14. Garnish chilled cheesecake with pecan halves.

Yield: One 9-inch cheesecake

Next time you are having guests over for lunch or dinner, why not make them feel like royalty by giving them cheesecake?

You would be following the perfect example of the Lord Mayor of London in offering such hospitality. He choose cheesecake as the dessert to be served to Queen Elizabeth II at the luncheon in honor of her coronation back in June 1952. The dessert was called "cheese tarts" and was named after the maids of honor at the court of Queen Elizabeth I.

The celebration cheesecakes served by the Lord Mayor have led to, so far, forty years of reign by Queen Elizabeth II . . . and your guests could enjoy both the cheesecake dessert and being "Queen (even if only) for a day."

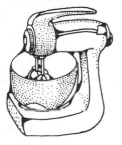

• PECAN PRALINE SUPERB •

Sandra Lucas Hurd
Southbury, Connecticut

Think of the combination of maple sugar and cheesecake covered with an elegant glazed topping and you will know that here is something no one can resist.

CRUST

1½ cups finely crushed shortbread
   cookie crumbs

¼ cup butter, melted
½ cup finely chopped pecans

FILLING

1½ pounds cream cheese, softened
1¼ cups light brown sugar
3 eggs, at room temperature

3 tablespoons flour
1½ teaspoons maple extract
½ cup chopped pecans

GLAZE

¼ cup pure maple syrup

12 to 14 pecan halves

1. Preheat oven to 350° F.

2. To make crust, combine cookie crumbs, butter, and pecans and press into the bottom and up the sides of a 9-inch springform pan.

3. Bake for 10 minutes, remove from oven, and set aside.

4. To make filling, with an electric mixer set on medium speed beat cream cheese and sugar until light and fluffy.

5. Add eggs, one at a time, beating well until smooth.

6. Blend in flour, maple extract, and pecans. Pour filling into crust.

7. Place a roasting pan filled with hot water on the bottom rack of the oven. Place cheesecake on middle rack of oven and bake for 50 to 60 minutes, until set.

8. Remove from oven and cool on a wire rack for 1 to 2 hours.

9. To make glaze, spoon 3 tablespoons of the maple syrup over top of cooled cheesecake.

10. Arrange pecan halves around edge and then, using a pastry brush, brush remaining maple syrup over pecans to make them shiny. Refrigerate for several hours.

Yield: One 9-inch cheesecake

⋅ CHOCOLATE ALMOND CHEESECAKE ⋅

Kim McPherson
Cary, North Carolina

Chocolate and amaretto cookies in both the crust and the filling plus a generous amount of marzipan will make this mouth-watering cheesecake disappear very quickly.

CRUST

1 ounce unsweetened chocolate	3 cups amaretto cookie crumbs
5 tablespoons butter	2 tablespoons sugar

FILLING

4 ounces marzipan, softened	½ cup sugar
¼ cup amaretto liqueur	4 eggs
6 ounces semi-sweet chocolate, melted	½ cup light cream
1½ pounds cream cheese, softened	1½ cups amaretto cookie crumbs

1. To make crust, melt chocolate and butter over low heat.
2. Remove from heat and mix in cookie crumbs and sugar.
3. Press into the bottom and 1 inch up the sides of a 9-inch springform pan. Set aside.

4. Preheat oven to 350° F.

5. To make filling, with an electric mixer set on medium speed beat marzipan and amaretto liqueur until smooth.

6. Add chocolate and beat until smooth again. Set aside.

7. Beat cream cheese until smooth.

8. Gradually beat in sugar until well combined.

9. Beat in eggs, one at a time.

10. Add cream and blend well.

11. Beat in marzipan mixture and then fold in cookie crumbs.

12. Pour filling into crust and bake for 1 hour and 10 minutes, or until set.

13. Remove from oven and let cool on a wire rack for 1 to 2 hours. Chill for at least 8 hours.

Yield: One 9-inch cheesecake

• CARAMEL PECAN LAYERS •

Mrs. C. E. Simmons
Booker, Texas

Just as archaeologists excavate layer by layer to discover ancient treasures, whoever eats this creamy caramel and nut cheesecake will discover layer after layer of culinary treasures.

CRUST

1½ cups graham cracker crumbs
⅓ cup butter or margarine, melted

¼ cup sugar
¼ cup finely ground pecans

FILLING

1½ pounds cream cheese, softened
¾ cup sugar
1 teaspoon vanilla
2 tablespoons flour
3 egg yolks

3 egg whites, beaten until stiff
½ cup prepared caramel sundae
   topping
½ cup chopped pecans

GLAZE

1½ teaspoons butter or margarine
1½ teaspoons water

1 tablespoon brown sugar
15 pecan halves

1. Preheat oven to 350° F.

2. To make crust, combine graham cracker crumbs, butter or margarine, sugar, and pecans and press into the bottom and up the sides of a 9-inch springform pan.

3. Bake for 8 minutes, remove from oven, and set aside.

4. Increase oven temperature to 450° F.

5. To make filling, with an electric mixer set on medium speed beat cream cheese, sugar, vanilla, and flour until well blended.

6. Add egg yolks, one at a time, mixing well after each addition.

7. Fold in egg whites.

8. Remove 1½ cups of the batter and set aside.

9. Mix caramel sundae topping into remaining batter. Pour into crust. Sprinkle chopped pecans over top. Carefully spread reserved batter over pecans.

10. Bake at 450° F. for 7 minutes.

11. Reduce oven temperature to 325° F. and bake for 50 minutes more.

12. Turn off oven, open oven door slightly, and let cheesecake sit in oven for 45 minutes.

13. Remove cheesecake from oven, let cool for 1 to 2 hours on a wire rack, and then remove rim of pan. Chill for 4 to 6 hours.

14. To make glaze, place butter or margarine, water, and brown sugar in a saucepan and heat to a boil.

15. Add pecan halves and cook for 2 minutes, stirring to coat pecan halves. Remove pecan halves from saucepan, letting syrup drippings fall into saucepan, and place on wax paper to cool.

16. Before serving, drizzle syrup in saucepan over top of chilled cheesecake. Arrange pecan halves on top.

Yield: One 9-inch cheesecake

• PAPAYA BURST •

Larry Mitchell
Caldwell, Idaho

This creamy papaya cheesecake sitting on a white chocolate crust and topped with macadamia nuts just bursts with fruity flavor.

CRUST

6 ounces white chocolate, melted

FILLING

1½ pounds cream cheese   *¾ cup sugar*
4 eggs   *1½ cups mashed papaya*

GARNISH

chopped macadamia nuts

1. To make crust, spread white chocolate onto the bottom of a well-buttered 9-inch springform pan. Set aside.
2. Preheat oven to 350 ° F.
3. To make filling, with an electric mixer set on medium speed beat cream cheese until smooth.

4. Add eggs, one at a time, beating well after each addition.
5. Beat in sugar.
6. Fold in papaya.
7. Pour filling into crust and bake for about 50 minutes, until edges are puffed and golden.
8. Remove from oven and let cool on a wire rack for 1 to 2 hours.
9. Remove rim of pan and chill for 4 to 6 hours.
10. Garnish chilled cheesecake with macadamia nuts.

Yield: One 9-inch cheesecake

• GINGER PEAR CHEESECAKE •

Roxanne E. Chan
Albany, California

Ginger and spice and everything nice, with a crispy, crunchy crust.

CRUST

1 cup flour
¼ cup sugar
½ teaspoon ground ginger

½ cup butter
½ cup ground pecans
1 egg, beaten

FILLING

1½ pounds cream cheese, softened
⅔ cup honey
4 eggs
1 tablespoon fresh lemon juice
1 tablespoon freshly grated ginger

1 cup coarsely grated pear
⅓ cup golden raisins
*¼ cup finely chopped crystallized
  ginger*

TOPPING

15 to 20 pecan halves

1. To make crust, combine flour, sugar, and ginger, mixing well.
2. Cut in butter until mixture resembles coarse crumbs.
3. Add pecans and egg and mix together well.
4. Press into the bottom and up the sides of a 9-inch springform pan. Chill.
5. Preheat oven to 350° F.
6. To make filling, with an electric mixer set on medium speed beat cream cheese, honey, eggs, lemon juice, and ginger until well blended.
7. Stir in pear, raisins, and crystallized ginger.
8. Pour filling into chilled crust and bake for 45 minutes. Remove from oven.
9. To make topping, arrange pecans on cheesecake and then bake for about 30 minutes more, until set.
10. Remove from oven and let cool on a wire rack for 1 to 2 hours. Chill for 4 to 6 hours.

Yield: One 9-inch cheesecake

• BLACK FOREST CHEESECAKE •

Sandra Krueger
Safety Harbor, Florida

Amaretto liqueur, cherries, and chocolate are all here in this version of a European legend.

CRUST

1½ cups graham cracker crumbs
⅓ cup butter or margarine, melted

¼ cup sugar
¼ cup cocoa powder

FILLING

1½ pounds cream cheese, softened
1½ cups sugar
4 eggs

¼ cup amaretto liqueur
¼ cup maraschino cherry juice

TOPPING

4 ounces semi-sweet chocolate, melted

½ cup sour cream

GARNISH

whipped cream

maraschino cherries with stems

1. To make crust, combine graham cracker crumbs, butter or margarine, sugar, and cocoa powder, mixing together well.

2. Firmly press into the bottom and 1 inch up the sides of a 9-inch springform pan. Set aside.

3. Preheat oven to 350° F.

4. To make filling, with an electric mixer set on medium speed beat cream cheese until fluffy.

5. Gradually add sugar, mixing in well.

6. Add eggs, one at a time, beating well after each addition.

7. Stir in amaretto liqueur and cherry juice until well blended.

8. Pour filling into crust and bake for 1 hour.

9. Remove from oven and cool 2 to 3 hours on a wire rack.

10. To make topping, combine melted chocolate and sour cream and spread evenly over top of cooled cheesecake.

11. Chill overnight.

12. Garnish chilled cheesecake with whipped cream and cherries.

Yield: One 9-inch cheesecake

• ORANGE POPPYSEED CHEESECAKE •

Tom Pacher
Everett, Washington

Combine four different orange flavors with poppyseeds and marzipan and you get a great-looking, great-tasting cheesecake that will win any contest.

CRUST

1⅔ cups graham crackers	½ cup unsalted butter, melted
½ cup chopped almonds	

FILLING

2 pounds cream cheese, softened	2 teaspoons fresh orange zest
1½ cups sugar	2 tablespoons almond extract
2 tablespoons flour	2 teaspoons orange flavoring
4 eggs, at room temperature	½ cup orange juice concentrate
½ cup heavy cream	3 tablespoons poppyseeds
2 ounces marzipan, softened	

TOPPING

⅔ cup heavy cream	¼ cup orange liqueur
⅓ cup sugar	

GARNISH

fresh orange zest   *slivered almond*

1. To make crust, combine graham cracker crumbs, almonds, and butter.
2. Pat into the bottom and up the sides of a buttered 9-inch springform pan. Set aside.
3. Preheat oven to 425° F.
4. To make filling, with an electric mixer set on medium speed beat cream cheese until smooth.
5. Add sugar and beat until light and fluffy.
6. Mix in flour.
7. Beat in eggs, mixing until smooth. Set aside.
8. Using a processor or blender, puree cream, marzipan, and orange zest.
9. Add to cheesecake batter and mix together well.
10. Mix in almond extract, orange flavoring, orange juice concentrate, and poppyseeds.
11. Pour batter into crust, place springform pan on a cookie sheet, and bake for 15 minutes.
12. Reduce oven temperature to 225° F. Bake for 1 hour and 10 minutes to 1 hour and 20 minutes more, until set.
13. Remove from oven and let cool on a wire rack for 1 to 2 hours. Refrigerate overnight.
14. To make topping, with an electric mixer set on high speed whip cream until just fluffy.
15. Add sugar and continue beating on high for 1 minute.

16. Add orange liqueur and whip briefly, until just blended. Spoon evenly over top of chilled cheesecake.

17. Garnish with orange zest and slivered almonds.

Yield: One 9-inch cheesecake

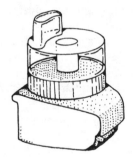

Some foods are cherished for nutrition, some for their taste or status, others for their connection to romantic memories. But to some food aficionados, a major attraction is the added element of the historical, cultural, and geographical mystique that surrounds a particular food.

Consider, for example, the column "Seasoned Cook—Chasing Cheesecake," written by Jim Villas for the "Man at His Best" section of *Esquire* magazine in the July 1982 issue. Mr. Villas writes that it can be weird eating cheesecake outside of New York City because it "just doesn't taste right—even when it's imported frozen from New York."

Mr. Villas goes on to describe the cheesecakes at various famous and renowned restaurants in Beverly Hills, Miami, and Newport, but, he writes, it's not the same. Perhaps it is not the same because "the water or altitude in these locations has some effect on the cake, or maybe there's something incongruent about eating cheesecake in surroundings that lack the proper noise level, aroma, and degree of human indifference that New Yorkers expect in a great deli or steak house. . . . New York cheesecake . . . is a food to be sought after and consumed only on its home territory."

Maybe they should call it "the Big Cheesecake" instead of "the Big Apple."

• CHOCOLATE FANTASY •

Sharla House
Gahanna, Ohio

Looking for an intense cheesecake with real chocolate enhanced by a hint of coffee? You've found it here!

CRUST

20 cream-filled chocolate sandwich
   cookies

3 tablespoons butter, softened
1 tablespoon sugar

FILLING

12 ounces semi-sweet chocolate
¼ cup coffee liqueur
2 tablespoons butter
2 eggs

⅓ cup sugar
¼ teaspoon salt
1 cup sour cream
1 pound cream cheese, softened

GARNISH

whipped cream

1. To make crust, place cookies, butter, and sugar in a food processor and pulse ingredients until mixture starts to hold its shape.

2. Press firmly into the bottom of a 9-inch springform pan. Set aside.

3. Preheat oven to 350° F.

4. To make filling, heat chocolate, liqueur, and butter over medium heat, stirring, until melted and smooth. Remove from heat and set aside.

5. With an electric mixer set on medium speed, beat together eggs, sugar, and salt.

6. Add sour cream, blending well.

7. Add cream cheese, a small piece at a time, beating until smooth.

8. Gradually blend in chocolate mixture. Pour filling into crust.

9. Place a pan of water on oven rack below cheesecake rack.

10. Bake for 50 minutes or until filling is barely set in the middle.

11. Remove from oven and let stand on a wire rack at room temperature for 1 hour.

12. Refrigerate for several hours or overnight to develop the chocolate flavor.

13. Garnish with whipped cream.

Yield: One 9-inch cheesecake

· OLD-FASHIONED GOODNESS ·

Theresa Charysyn
Tucson, Arizona

A light, lemon-flavored, traditional, crustless cheesecake that will be a nostalgic favorite . . . and so easy to make.

1 pound cream cheese
1½ cups cottage cheese
1½ cups sugar
4 eggs, well beaten
2 tablespoons fresh lemon juice
1 teaspoon vanilla

3 tablespoons flour
3 tablespoons cornstarch
½ cup butter, melted
2 cups sour cream
1 teaspoon fresh lemon zest

1. Preheat oven to 325° F.
2. With an electric mixer set on medium speed, beat cream cheese until light and fluffy.
3. Strain cottage cheese through a fine sieve into the cream cheese.
4. Gradually beat in sugar, eggs, lemon juice, and vanilla.
5. Mix together flour and cornstarch and gradually beat into the cheese mixture.
6. Add butter and sour cream, mixing well.
7. Fold in lemon zest.
8. Pour batter into a greased 9-inch springform pan and bake for 1 hour and 10 minutes, or until set in center.

9. Turn off oven and let cake cool in oven for 2 hours.

10. Remove from oven and let cake cool on a wire rack for 1 to 2 hours.

11. Chill for 4 to 6 hours. Make sure cheesecake is chilled thoroughly before removing rim of pan.

Yield: One 9-inch cheesecake

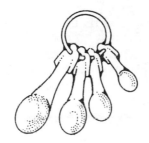

· DATE 'N' NUT CHEESECAKE ·

Sophia Benfield
Valparaiso, Indiana

Dates and nuts combine with coffee to make this cheesecake a real "eye-opener."

CRUST

⅓ cup margarine	1 egg
⅓ cup sugar	1¼ cups flour

FILLING

½ cup water	2 eggs
1 tablespoon instant coffee powder	½ cup light cream
1 cup finely chopped dates	1 cup finely chopped walnuts or
1 pound cream cheese, softened	pecans
½ cup sugar	1 tablespoon coffee liqueur
1 teaspoon vanilla	

1. Preheat oven to 450° F.
2. To make crust, with an electric mixer on medium speed cream margarine and sugar until light and fluffy.
3. Blend in egg.

4. Add flour, mixing well until a soft dough is formed.

5. Press into the bottom and 1½ inches up the sides of a greased 9-inch springform pan.

6. Bake for 5 minutes. Remove from oven and let cool.

7. Reduce oven temperature to 425° F.

8. To make filling, in a saucepan heat water to boiling: stir in coffee and dates.

9. Reduce heat and simmer for 5 minutes, stirring constantly.

10. Remove from heat and set aside to cool.

11. With an electric mixer set on medium speed, beat cream cheese, sugar, and vanilla until well blended.

12. Add eggs, mixing well.

13. Blend in cream.

14. Add coffee mixture, chopped nuts, and coffee liqueur, blending well.

15. Pour filling into crust and bake for 10 minutes.

16. Reduce oven temperature to 350° F. and bake for about 50 minutes more, until set.

17. Remove from oven, let cool slightly, and loosen rim of pan.

18. Let cool on a wire rack for 1 to 2 hours before removing rim.

19. Chill for 4 to 6 hours.

Yield: One 9-inch cheesecake

• BRANDY CHOCOLATE SWIRL •

Mrs. Lois M. Clonts
Bakersfield, California

The chocolate and brandy join together in this cheesecake to give truly intense chocolate satisfaction.

CRUST

1¼ cups graham cracker crumbs
3 tablespoons sugar

3 tablespoons margarine, melted

FILLING

6 ounces semi-sweet chocolate
½ cup sugar
1 pound cream cheese, softened
¾ cup sugar
½ cup sour cream

2 tablespoons flour
1 teaspoon vanilla
¼ cup brandy
4 eggs
½ cup finely chopped walnuts

1. To make crust, combine graham cracker crumbs, sugar, and margarine, mixing together well.

2. Pat firmly into the bottom and 1 inch up the sides of a 9-inch springform pan. Set aside.

3. Preheat oven to 325° F.

4. To make filling, combine chocolate and ½ cup sugar in the top of a double boiler, heat gently over hot water until chocolate melts, and then stir until smooth. Remove from heat and set aside.

5. With an electric mixer set on medium speed, beat cream cheese until light and creamy.

6. Gradually beat in ¾ cup sugar.

7. Mix in sour cream, flour, vanilla, and brandy.

8. Add eggs, one at a time, beating after each addition.

9. Fold in chopped walnuts.

10. Divide the batter in half and stir the chocolate mixture into one of the halves. Pour into crust and then pour in the remaining half of the batter. Using a knife, swirl chocolate batter through the plain batter to marbleize.

11. Bake for about 50 minutes, until only a 3-inch circle in the center will shake.

12. Remove from oven and let cool on a wire rack for 1 to 2 hours. Chill for 4 to 6 hours.

Yield: One 9-inch cheesecake

◆ LAST WEEKEND'S CARAMEL CHOCOLATE ◆ CHUNK CHEESECAKE

Penni Mallen Deutsch
Ft. Lauderdale, Florida

A scrumptious crust that is not to be believed holds a cheesecake with delicate caramel flavor and topped with chocolate that you will want to believe . . . last weekend, this weekend, and every weekend evermore.

CRUST

¾ cup quick rolled oats
¾ cup chopped pecans
¾ cup light brown sugar

½ teaspoon cinnamon
¼ cup butter, melted

FILLING

1½ pounds cream cheese, softened
⅓ cup dark brown sugar
⅓ cup dark corn syrup
5 teaspoons cornstarch

3 eggs
1 egg yolk
1½ teaspoons vanilla
1 cup chocolate chunks

1. Preheat oven to 350° F.
2. To make crust, mix together oats, pecans, brown sugar, and cinnamon.
3. Add butter, mixing well.

4. Press into the bottom of a greased 9-inch springform pan.

5. Bake for 15 to 18 minutes, until golden, remove from oven, and set aside to cool.

6. To make filling, with an electric mixer set on medium speed combine cream cheese, brown sugar, corn syrup, and cornstarch, beating well.

7. Add eggs and egg yolk, beating well.

8. Mix in vanilla.

9. Pour filling into crust and bake for 15 minutes.

10. Reduce oven temperature to 225° F. and bake for 40 minutes more.

11. Remove from oven and sprinkle chocolate chunks over top.

12. Bake again at 225° F. for 35 minutes. Turn off oven and leave cheesecake in oven for 1 hour more.

13. Remove from oven, let cool on a wire rack for 1 to 2 hours, and chill uncovered overnight.

Yield: One 9-inch cheesecake

⋅ VERY, VERY IRISH CREAM ⋅

Suzan Spafford Hartnagle
Syracuse, New York

A heavenly, smooth cheesecake that tastes just like you poured it out of a bottle of good Irish cream liqueur.

CRUST

2 cups graham cracker crumbs
½ cup finely ground almonds

½ cup sugar
½ butter, melted

FILLING

2 pounds cream cheese, softened
1 cup sugar
1 teaspoon vanilla

¾ Irish cream liqueur
3 eggs

TOPPING

1 cup sour cream
¼ cup Irish cream liqueur

¼ cup sugar

1. To make crust, combine graham cracker crumbs, almonds, and sugar, mixing well.

2. Stir in butter.

3. Pat into the bottom and up the sides of a 9-inch springform pan. Place pan in freezer until filling is ready.

4. Preheat oven to 350° F.

5. To make filling, with an electric mixer set on medium speed beat cream cheese and sugar until smooth.

6. Add in vanilla and Irish cream liqueur; blend well.

7. Add eggs, one at a time, blending well after each addition.

8. Pour filling into crust and bake for 40 minutes. Remove from oven and set aside.

9. To make topping, whisk together sour cream, Irish cream liqueur, and sugar. Pour over top of cheesecake, spreading evenly.

10. Return cheesecake to oven and bake for 5 minutes more.

11. Remove from oven, let cool on a wire rack for 1 to 2 hours, and chill for 4 to 6 hours.

Yield: One 9-inch cheesecake

· CHOCOLATE-ORANGE CHEESECAKE ·

Carole A. Resnick
Cleveland Heights, Ohio

It's chocolate! It's orange! It's everything you want in a cheesecake, with a great combination of tastes . . . and a cookie crust.

CRUST

1 cup chocolate wafer crumbs
3 tablespoons unsalted butter, melted and cooled

1 tablespoon fresh orange zest
1/4 teaspoon cinnamon

FILLING

2 pounds cream cheese, softened
3/4 cup sugar
4 extra-large eggs, at room temperature
1/2 cup sour cream
1 teaspoon vanilla

4 ounces semi-sweet or bittersweet chocolate, melted and cooled
2 tablespoons orange-flavored liqueur or 3 tablespoons frozen orange juice concentrate
2 teaspoons fresh orange zest

TOPPING

whipped cream
fresh orange zest

orange slices

1. Preheat oven to 325° F.
2. To make crust, combine wafer crumbs, butter, orange zest, and cinnamon.
3. Press into the bottom of a 9-inch springform pan.
4. Bake for 10 minutes, remove from oven, and set aside.
5. Increase oven temperature to 350° F.
6. To make filling, with an electric mixer set on medium speed combine cream cheese and sugar, beating until smooth and well blended.
7. Add eggs, one at a time, beating well after each addition.
8. Add sour cream and vanilla. Mix well.
9. Pour 3 cups of batter into another bowl and add the chocolate to this portion of the batter. Mix until well blended.
10. Pour chocolate batter into crust.
11. Place springform pan into a large roasting pan and fill roasting pan with boiling water that reaches halfway up the sides of the springform pan.
12. Bake for 30 minutes.
13. While cheesecake is baking, add orange liqueur (or orange juice concentrate) and orange zest to remaining batter.
14. Remove cheesecake from oven and reduce oven temperature to 325° F.
15. Spoon remaining batter over top of cheesecake, spreading evenly.
16. Return cheesecake to roasting pan and bake for an additional 30 minutes. Check water level in roasting pan and add more water if necessary.
17. Turn off oven. Allow cheesecake to cool in oven with door closed for 1 hour.
18. Remove springform pan from oven and roasting pan and let cool on a wire rack for 1 to 2 hours. Loosen cake from sides of pan. Remove rim and chill for at least 4 hours.

19. Remove cake from refrigerator 30 minutes before serving.

20. To make topping, mix together whipped cream and orange zest and spoon over top of chilled cheesecake. Arrange orange slices on top.

Yield: One 9-inch cheesecake

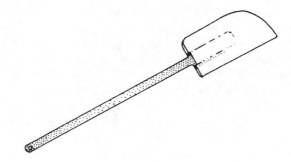

The list of contributions by immigrants to the growth and success of the United States is quite long and varied, but is there any greater contribution on that list than cheesecake?

Cheesecake in the United States really began around 1900 with two types that became popular among immigrants in New York City. There was Jewish cheesecake, having a smooth filling made with cream cheese, and Italian cheesecake, which used ricotta cheese in its filling.

Over the last century these two basic types of cheesecakes have grown in popularity among all ethnic groups and have spawned countless variations with mind-stretching combinations of ingredients that would, no doubt, be a great source of interest and amusement to those early Jewish and Italian bakers.

• MOCHA RUM CHEESECAKE •

Cecelia Rooney
Point Pleasant, New Jersey

Think how good chocolate, coffee, and rum would be when surrounded by an oatmeal cookie crust and then you will know what a superb cheesecake this is.

CRUST

1½ cups crisp oatmeal cookie crumbs   ¼ cup butter or margarine, melted

FILLING

¼ cup rum
1 tablespoon instant coffee crystals
1½ pounds cream cheese, softened
1 cup sugar
4 ounces semi-sweet chocolate,
    melted and cooled

2 tablespoons flour
1 teaspoon vanilla
3 eggs

GARNISH

whipped cream   raspberries
chocolate curls

1. To make crust, mix together cookie crumbs and butter or margarine.

2. Press into the bottom and 1½ inches up the sides of a 9-inch springform pan. Set aside.

3. Preheat oven to 350° F.

4. To make filling, with an electric mixer set on medium speed stir together rum and coffee crystals. Set aside.

5. Beat together cream cheese, sugar, melted chocolate, flour, and vanilla.

6. Add eggs, all at once, beating until just combined. Do not overbeat.

7. Stir in rum mixture.

8. Pour filling into crust and bake for about 50 minutes, until center appears to be set.

9. Remove from oven and let cool for 10 minutes.

10. Loosen sides of cheesecake from pan and remove rim. Let cheesecake stand on a wire rack at room temperature for 2 hours, or until cool.

11. Chill for 4 to 6 hours.

12. Garnish chilled cheesecake with whipped cream, chocolate curls, and raspberries.

Yield: One 9-inch cheesecake

• DESERT STORM •

Shelley Anderson
Sterling, Illinois

Deserving to be as popular and patriotic as Ma's apple pie, Desert Storm cheesecake is like a creamy apple-cinnamon coffee cake . . . and it will truly arouse your spirits.

CRUST

1 cup graham cracker crumbs
3 tablespoons sugar
½ teaspoon cinnamon

¼ cup butter, melted
½ cup chopped walnuts

FILLING

1 pound cream cheese, softened
½ cup sugar
2 eggs
½ teaspoon vanilla

4 cups very thin apple slices
⅓ cup sugar
½ teaspoon cinnamon
½ cup chopped walnuts

1. Preheat oven to 350° F.
2. To make crust, combine graham cracker crumbs, sugar, cinnamon, butter, and walnuts.
3. Press mixture into the bottom of a 9-inch springform pan.

4. Bake for 5 minutes, remove pan from oven, and set aside. (If a chewier crust is desired, do not bake the crust separately.)

5. To make filling, with an electric mixer set on medium speed combine cream cheese and ½ cup sugar, mixing until creamy.

6. Add eggs, one at a time, mixing well after each addition.

7. Blend in vanilla and pour filling into crust. Set aside.

8. Toss apple slices with ⅓ cup sugar and cinnamon.

9. Spoon coated apple slices over filling and then sprinkle with walnuts.

10. Bake for approximately 1 hour.

11. Remove pan from oven, loosen cake from sides of pan, and let cool in pan on a wire rack for 1 to 2 hours.

12. Chill in refrigerator for 4 to 6 hours.

Yield: One 9-inch cheesecake

· CHOCOLATE 1-2-3 SURPRISE ·

Hilary McLaughlin
Boston, Massachusetts

Who hasn't been told to count to three and then there will be a surprise? Here is the best 1-2-3 surprise ever, with three layers lusciously combining chocolate and almonds.

CRUST

1 cup graham cracker crumbs
¼ cup ground almonds
2½ tablespoons butter, melted

2 teaspoons almond extract
¼ cup sugar

FILLING

1½ pounds cream cheese, softened
3 eggs
¾ cup sugar
1 teaspoon vanilla
1 teaspoon almond extract
2 tablespoons amaretto liqueur

2 ounces semi-sweet chocolate, melted
3 ounces white chocolate, melted
2 ounces unsweetened chocolate, melted

GARNISH

white chocolate shavings

1. To make crust, combine graham cracker crumbs, ground almonds, butter, almond extract, and sugar.

2. Press into the bottom and 1 inch up the sides of a greased 9-inch springform pan. Set aside.

3. Preheat oven to 250° F.

4. To make filling, beat cream cheese until light and fluffy and then add eggs, one at a time.

5. Mix in sugar and vanilla. Divide batter equally into three bowls.

6. Stir almond extract, 1 tablespoon of the amaretto liqueur, and semi-sweet chocolate into ⅓ of the batter. Pour into the crust.

7. Stir white chocolate into another ⅓ of the batter and carefully pour over semi-sweet chocolate layer.

8. Stir unsweetened chocolate and remaining 1 tablespoon of the amaretto liqueur into the last ⅓ of the batter and gently pour over white chocolate layer.

9. Bake for 1½ hours.

10. Remove from oven, let cool on a wire rack for 1 to 2 hours, and then chill in refrigerator for 4 to 6 hours.

11. Garnish chilled cheesecake with white chocolate shavings.

Yield: One 9-inch cheesecake

• CHOCOLATE TURTLE •

Rose H. Ryczkowski
De Pere, Wisconsin

Creamy, crunchy, and chewy . . . this is really a special treat for caramel and chocolate lovers.

CRUST

6 tablespoons margarine, melted   2 cups vanilla wafer crumbs

FILLING

1 pound caramel candies   ½ cup sugar
¾ cup evaporated milk   2 eggs
1¼ cups coarsely chopped pecans   4 ounces chocolate, melted
1 pound cream cheese, softened

1. Preheat oven to 350° F.
2. To make crust, combine margarine and wafer crumbs and pat into the bottom of a 9-inch springform pan.
3. Bake for 5 minutes.
4. Remove pan from oven and set aside.
5. To make filling, place caramel candies and evaporated milk in a heavy

saucepan and cook over medium-high heat, stirring occasionally, until caramels are melted.

6. Remove pan from heat and pour filling into crust. Sprinkle pecans over top. Set aside.

7. With an electric mixer set on medium speed, beat together cream cheese and sugar.

8. Add eggs, one at a time, and mix in melted chocolate. Pour over pecans and smooth out.

9. Bake for 40 minutes.

10. Remove pan from oven and let cool on a wire rack for 1 to 2 hours.

11. Chill for 4 to 6 hours.

Yield: One 9-inch cheesecake

• TRI-COLORED ITALIAN CHEESECAKE •

Elaine Sanchez-Crescenzo
Hollywood, Florida

Beauty is more than skin-deep in this attractive cheesecake with three layers of different colors and three deliciously different tastes.

CRUST

½ cup flour
¼ cup butter

¼ cup walnuts
1 tablespoon sugar

FILLING

CHOCOLATE LAYER
11 ounces cream cheese, softened
2 eggs
½ cup sugar

¼ cup cocoa powder
½ teaspoon vanilla
¼ cup mini chocolate chips

ALMOND LAYER
11 ounces cream cheese, softened
3 tablespoons heavy cream
½ teaspoon almond extract

2 eggs
½ cup sugar

FRUIT LAYER

11 ounces cream cheese, softened
2 eggs
5 drops red food coloring

½ cup sugar
1½ cups sour cherries, drained

TOPPING

½ cup sour cream
½ cup sugar

1 teaspoon vanilla

1. Preheat oven to 350° F.
2. To make crust blend together flour, butter, walnuts, and sugar.
3. Press mixture into the bottom of a 9-inch springform pan.
4. Bake for about 15 minutes, until golden brown.
5. Remove from oven and cool on rack while preparing chocolate layer.
6. To make chocolate layer, in a food processor blend together cream cheese, eggs, sugar, cocoa powder, and vanilla.
7. Fold in chocolate chips. Pour into crust.
8. Bake for 20 to 25 minutes, until chocolate layer is set.
9. Remove from oven and cool on a wire rack while preparing almond layer.
10. To make almond layer, in a food processor puree cream cheese, heavy cream, and almond extract.
11. Add eggs and sugar, blending until smooth.
12. Carefully spoon almond mixture over cooled chocolate layer, spreading evenly.

13. Return to oven and bake for about 25 minutes, until almond layer is set.

14. Remove from oven and cool on a wire rack while preparing fruit layer.

15. To make fruit layer blend together cream cheese, sugar, eggs, and food coloring.

16. Fold in cherries and then spoon carefully on top of cooled almond layer, spreading evenly.

17. Return to oven and bake at 350° F. for about 30 minutes, until center of fruit layer is set.

18. Remove from oven and let cool slightly on a wire rack.

19. To make topping, mix together sour cream, sugar, and vanilla.

20. Carefully spread on top of cheesecake and return to oven, baking at 350° F. for 8 minutes.

21. Remove from oven and let cool 2 to 3 hours on a wire rack. Serve at room temperature.

Yield: One 9-inch cheesecake

• SNICKERS CHEESECAKE •

Tess Asiala
Calabasas, California

All the good things—peanuts, caramel, and chocolate—that have made Snickers candy bars so popular are right here in this cheesecake.

CRUST

1½ cups chocolate wafer crumbs   *¼ cup butter, melted*

FILLING

1½ pounds cream cheese, softened   *1 cup heavy cream*
1 cup sugar   *1½ cups small pieces of snack-*
4 eggs   *   sized Snickers candy bars*
1 tablespoon vanilla

TOPPING

4½ cups small pieces of snack-
*   sized Snickers candy bars*

FUDGE SAUCE

2 ounces unsweetened chocolate

3/4 cup sugar

1/3 cup boiling water

2 tablespoons butter

3 tablespoons light corn syrup

GARNISH

whipped cream

1. To make crust, combine wafer crumbs and butter.
2. Press into the bottom and up the sides of a 9½-inch springform pan. Set aside.
3. Preheat oven to 325° F.
4. To make filling, with an electric mixer set on medium speed combine cream cheese and sugar, beating until smooth.
5. Add in eggs, one at a time.
6. Add vanilla and heavy cream. Beat at medium speed for 5 minutes.
7. Fold in Snickers candy bar pieces.
8. Pour filling into crust and bake for 1 hour and 20 minutes, or until cheesecake is almost set in center.
9. Remove from oven and let cool on a wire rack for 1 to 2 hours.
10. Top cooled cheesecake with Snickers candy bar pieces and chill for 4 to 6 hours.
11. To make fudge sauce, combine chocolate and butter in a heavy saucepan and cook over low heat, stirring gently, until mixture has melted.
12. Stir in boiling water, sugar, and light corn syrup, mixing until smooth.

13. Increase heat to medium and stir until mixture starts to boil.

14. Reduce heat and let simmer for 5 minutes without stirring.

15. Remove from heat and let cool for 15 to 20 minutes. Drizzle over chilled cheesecake just before serving.

16. Garnish with whipped cream.

Yield: One 9½-inch cheesecake

• BANANA SPLIT •

Mrs. Judy Anderson
Johnstown, Ohio

There are two ways to serve this cheesecake delight: as a sophisticated dessert with just the pineapple on top or, to recapture your childhood memories of the ice cream parlor, as a new version of the classic sundae with all the old-fashioned trimmings.

CRUST

1½ cups chocolate wafer crumbs
2 tablespoons sugar

6 tablespoons margarine, melted

FILLING

1 pound cream cheese, softened
1¼ cups sugar
2½ tablespoons cornstarch
3 eggs
1¼ teaspoons vanilla

1 cup sour cream
2 tablespoons fresh lemon juice
1 cup pureed bananas
dash of salt

TOPPING

½ cup sugar
3 tablespoons cornstarch

2½ cups crushed pineapple,
   undrained

GARNISH

whipped cream
chocolate syrup

chopped peanuts
maraschino cherries

1. Preheat oven to 300° F.
2. To make crust, combine wafer crumbs, sugar, and margarine.
3. Press into the bottom of a 9½-inch springform pan.
4. Bake for 5 minutes. Remove from oven and set aside.
5. To make filling, with an electric mixer set on medium speed beat cream cheese until smooth.
6. Gradually add sugar and cornstarch.
7. Beat in eggs, one at a time, mixing well after each addition.
8. Beat in vanilla, sour cream, lemon juice, bananas, and salt.
9. Pour filling into crust and bake for 1 hour and 10 minutes.
10. Turn off oven and let cheesecake set in warm oven for 30 minutes.
11. Remove from oven and let cool on a wire rack for 1 to 2 hours.
12. Refrigerate until well chilled—6 hours or overnight.
13. To make topping, mix sugar and cornstarch in a saucepan.
14. Add pineapple and then cook over medium heat until thick.
15. Remove from heat and let cool.
16. Spread evenly over top of cooled cheesecake.
17. Refrigerate until chilled.
18. Garnish with whipped cream, chocolate syrup, peanuts, and cherries.

Yield: One 9½-inch cheesecake

The most famous of all English diaries is the one kept by Samuel Pepys during the seventeenth century. He was a member of the British parliament and a president of the Royal Society, an organization that encourages scientific research, publishes its *Proceedings* and *Philosophical Transactions*, and advises the British government on scientific matters.

Mr. Pepys's diary offers not only an intimate record of his private life from January 1, 1660, to May 31, 1669, but also an insightful picture of social life and conditions during that period, including the plague of 1665 and the Great London Fire the following year.

Included among Pepys's most noteworthy observations and experiences chronicling English life during that period was the entry for August 11, 1667:

"We . . . eat some of the best cheese-cakes that I ever eat in my life."

Even back then, over three hundred years ago, a good cheesecake was something not only to enjoy, but also to record as an important event.

Ten-Inch and Ten-and-a-Half-Inch Cheesecakes

• CREAMY NUTTY PUMPKIN CHEESECAKE •

Kathleen Winiski-Noel
East Windsor, New Jersey

This dessert is smooth, creamy, and high . . . the perfect pumpkin lover's cheesecake.

CRUST

1 cup ground pecans
1 cup ground macadamia nuts
2 tablespoons light brown sugar
1 egg white, beaten until frothy

1 teaspoon ground ginger
1 teaspoon finely grated fresh
   lemon zest

FILLING

2½ pounds cream cheese, softened
1 cup sugar
4 large eggs, lightly beaten
3 egg yolks, lightly beaten
3 tablespoons flour
2 teaspoons cinnamon
1 teaspoon ground cloves

1 teaspoon ground ginger
2 teaspoons finely grated fresh
   lemon zest
1 cup heavy cream
1 tablespoon vanilla
1⅔ cups pumpkin puree

GARNISH

fresh lemon zest curls or nutmeg

1. To make crust, thoroughly mix together pecans, macadamia nuts, brown sugar, egg white, ginger, and lemon zest.
2. Press into the bottom and up the sides of a 10-inch springform pan. Set aside.
3. Preheat oven to 425° F.
4. To make filling, with an electric mixer set on medium speed beat together cream cheese, sugar, eggs, and egg yolks.
5. Add flour, cinnamon, cloves, ginger, and lemon zest, mixing well.
6. Stir in cream and vanilla.
7. Add pumpkin and beat until thoroughly mixed.
8. Pour filling into crust and bake for 15 minutes.
9. Reduce oven temperature to 275° F. and bake for 1 hour longer.
10. Turn off oven and let cheesecake cool in oven for 8 hours.
11. Remove from oven and chill for several hours.
12. Garnish chilled cheesecake with lemon zest curls or dust lightly with nutmeg.

Yield: One 10-inch cheesecake

• SOUTHERN SWEET POTATO CHEESECAKE •

Joyce Mathis
Macon, Georgia

Sweet potatoes along with pumpkin pie spice and pecans provide southern hospitality in this cheesecake.

CRUST

*1½ cups finely crushed vanilla
   wafer crumbs*

*¾ cup finely chopped pecans
¼ cup butter, softened*

FILLING

*2 pounds cream cheese, softened
1½ cups sugar
5 eggs
1½ teaspoons pumpkin pie spice
2 cups sour cream*

*1 cup heavy cream
1 pound cooked sweet potatoes,
   mashed
1 teaspoon fresh lemon zest
¼ cup flour*

GARNISH

pecan halves

1. To make crust, combine wafer crumbs, pecans, and butter, crumbling together with fingers.

2. Press into the bottom and partway up the sides of a 10-inch springform pan. Set aside.

3. Preheat oven to 275° F.

4. To make filling, with an electric mixer set on medium speed beat cream cheese with sugar, eggs, pumpkin pie spice, sour cream, heavy cream, sweet potatoes, lemon zest, and flour. Blend together well.

5. Pour filling into crust and bake for about 2½ hours, until knife tests clean in center.

6. Remove from oven, let cool on a wire rack for 2 to 3 hours, and then refrigerate overnight.

7. Garnish with pecan halves.

Yield: One 10-inch cheesecake

⋅ UNCLE RONNIE'S BLUE-RIBBON APPLE ⋅
AND SPICE CHEESECAKE

Ron Findley
Newtown, Connecticut

A blue ribbon means a "winner," and the smooth texture and emphatically cinnamon-apple flavor bring victory to this cheesecake.

CRUST

1½ tablespoons butter, softened   *¾ cup graham cracker crumbs*

FILLING

3 pounds cream cheese, softened   *6 eggs*
2¾ cups sugar   *6 egg yolks*
¼ teaspoon salt   *2½ cups apple pie filling*
5 tablespoons cornstarch   *½ cup cinnamon*
¾ cup light cream   *1 tablespoon nutmeg*
2 tablespoons vanilla

1. To make crust, coat the bottom and sides of a 10-inch springform pan with butter.
2. Roll graham cracker crumbs to coat pan. Set aside.
3. Preheat oven to 325° F.

4. To make filling, with an electric mixer set on medium speed beat cream cheese until fluffy.

5. In a separate bowl, using an electric mixer set on medium speed, mix together sugar, salt, and cornstarch and add to cream cheese, blending well.

6. Stir in cream and vanilla, beating thoroughly.

7. Using an electric mixer set on medium speed, mix eggs and egg yolks together and then blend into cream cheese mixture.

8. Mix together apple pie filling, cinnamon, and nutmeg and then add to batter.

9. Pour filling into crust and bake for about 1 hour and 40 minutes. Cheesecake will rise very high.

10. Turn off oven, open door, and let cheesecake sit in oven to cool until cheesecake drops.

11. Remove from oven and let cool on a wire rack for 1 hour.

12. Remove rim of pan and chill for 4 to 6 hours.

Yield: One 10-inch cheesecake

• THE COLONEL'S CHEESECAKE •

Linda J. Thorpe
Honolulu, Hawaii

Good looks, good taste . . . here is a delightfully rich cheesecake that includes crushed cookies in the filling and a chocolate glaze on top.

CRUST

1¼ cups graham cracker crumbs
⅓ cup unsalted butter, melted

¼ cup firmly packed light brown sugar
1 teaspoon cinnamon

FILLING

2 pounds cream cheese, softened
1¼ cups sugar
2 tablespoons flour
4 extra-large eggs
2 large egg yolks
⅓ cup heavy cream

1 teaspoon vanilla
1½ cups chocolate cream sandwich cookie crumbs
2 cups sour cream
¼ cup sugar
1 teaspoon vanilla

GLAZE

½ cup heavy cream   1 teaspoon vanilla
4 ounces semi-sweet chocolate

GARNISH

5 chocolate cream sandwich
  cookies, cut in half

1. To make crust, combine graham cracker crumbs, butter, brown sugar, and cinnamon.
2. Press into the bottom and up the sides of a 10-inch springform pan.
3. Refrigerate for about 30 minutes, until firm.
4. Preheat oven to 425° F.
5. To make filling, with an electric mixer set on low speed beat cream cheese until smooth.
6. Beat in 1¼ cups sugar.
7. Add flour, mixing well.
8. Beat in eggs and egg yolks, until smooth.
9. Stir in heavy cream and 1 teaspoon vanilla.
10. Pour half of batter into crust and sprinkle with cookie crumbs.
11. Pour remaining batter over cookie crumbs, smoothing out with a spatula.
12. Bake for 15 minutes.
13. Reduce oven temperature to 225° F. and bake for another 50 minutes.

Loosely cover top of cheesecake with foil during second baking period if it is browning too quickly.

14. Remove from oven and increase oven temperature to 350° F.

15. Using an electric mixer set on medium speed, blend together sour cream, ¼ cup sugar, and 1 teaspoon vanilla and spread evenly over top of cheesecake.

16. Return to oven and bake at 350° F. for 7 minutes.

17. Remove from oven and immediately cover and refrigerate overnight.

18. To make glaze, scald cream in a heavy saucepan over high heat.

19. Add chocolate and vanilla, stirring for 1 minute.

20. Remove from heat and stir until chocolate has melted.

21. Refrigerate for 10 minutes.

22. Remove chilled cheesecake from refrigerator, uncover, and remove rim of pan.

23. Pour glaze over cheesecake.

24. Garnish with cookie halves, arranged cut side down, around edge of cake.

Yield: One 10-inch cheesecake

Cream cheese, the most commonly used ingredient in cheesecakes, was developed by an upstate New York farmer in the 1870s. It was later given the brand name "Philadelphia Cream Cheese" not because of any connection with the City of Brotherly Love in Pennsylvania, but because Philadelphia was known as a place of good taste and quality, especially for foods . . . and especially for dairy products.

⋄ OLD-FASHIONED RICOTTA CHEESECAKE ⋄

Tina E. Meyers
Fairport, New York

A truly traditional classic—Italian cheesecake—with the added goodness of honey.

Crust

1¼ cups graham cracker crumbs
¼ cup sugar

⅓ cup butter, softened

Filling

1⅔ cups ricotta cheese
1 pound cream cheese, softened
½ cup sugar
1 cup honey
4 large eggs

⅓ cup cornstarch
1 teaspoon vanilla
2 tablespoons fresh lemon juice
½ cup margarine, melted
2 cups sour cream

1. To make crust, combine graham cracker crumbs, sugar, and butter and press into the bottom and up the sides of a 10-inch springform pan.
2. Preheat oven to 325° F.
3. To make filling, with an electric mixer set on medium speed combine ricotta cheese and cream cheese, mixing together well.

4. Beat in sugar, honey, eggs, cornstarch, vanilla, lemon juice, margarine, and sour cream.

5. Pour filling into crust and bake for 1 hour and 10 minutes.

6. Turn off oven and let cheesecake set in oven for 2 hours. Do not open oven door.

7. Remove from oven and chill for 4 to 6 hours.

Yield: One 10-inch cheesecake

• RASPBERRY-ALMOND KEYS-CAKE •

Lisa Keys
Middlebury, Connecticut

From the fresh raspberry and yogurt topping down to the crunchy almond crust, here is one cheesecake that should not be missed.

CRUST

1½ cups vanilla cookie crumbs
1 cup chopped almonds

3 tablespoons almond paste
¼ cup unsalted butter, melted

FILLING

1½ pounds cream cheese, softened
¾ cup sugar
3 eggs

¼ cup raspberry liqueur
¼ cup Irish cream liqueur

TOPPING

1 cup raspberry yogurt

½ cup plain yogurt

GARNISH

1 ounce white chocolate, grated   *whole almonds*
whole fresh raspberries

1. To make crust, in a food processor combine cookie crumbs, almonds, and almond paste.
2. Pulse several times and then add butter. Pulse until evenly moist.
3. Press into the bottom and 1½ inches up the sides of a greased 10-inch springform pan.
4. Refrigerate while preparing filling.
5. Preheat oven to 325° F.
6. To make filling, with an electric mixer set on medium speed beat cream cheese and sugar until smooth.
7. Beat in eggs, raspberry liqueur, and Irish cream liqueur.
8. Pour filling into crust and bake for about 50 minutes, until center is just about set.
9. Remove from oven and cool on a wire rack.
10. To make topping, combine raspberry yogurt and plain yogurt and spread evenly over cooled cheesecake.
11. Refrigerate for about 6 hours.
12. Garnish with white chocolate, raspberries, and almonds.

Yield: One 10-inch cheesecake

• EUROPEAN CHEESECAKE •

Sharon Congdon
Vestal, New York

For those who prefer a Continental accent, this Stilton blue cheese cake is in the European tradition of sophisticated desserts.

CRUST

½ cup unsalted butter, melted
1½ cups coarsely chopped walnuts
½ cup graham cracker crumbs

¼ cup sugar
1 teaspoon cinnamon

FILLING

2 pounds cream cheese, softened
2 tablespoons flour
1 cup sugar
3 eggs, at room temperature

2 egg yolks, at room temperature
1 teaspoon vanilla
8 ounces Stilton blue cheese,
   crumbled into small pieces

TOPPING

1 tablespoon unsalted butter,
   melted

½ cup black walnut halves
dash of salt

1. Preheat oven to 350° F.

2. To make crust, mix together butter, walnuts, graham cracker crumbs, sugar, and cinnamon.

3. Press mixture into the bottom and up the sides of a buttered 10-inch springform pan. Chill for 10 minutes.

4. Bake for 8 to 10 minutes.

5. Remove from oven and let cool on a wire rack.

6. Wrap bottom and sides of pan with foil. Set aside.

7. To make filling, with an electric mixer set on medium speed beat cream cheese until smooth.

8. Add flour and sugar and beat together.

9. Add eggs, one at a time, beating well after each addition.

10. Add egg yolks and beat well.

11. Thoroughly mix in vanilla and blue cheese, and pour filling into crust.

12. Place springform pan into a large roasting pan containing enough hot water so water level comes halfway up the sides of the springform.

13. Bake for 1½ hours.

14. When baking is finished, turn off oven and leave cheesecake in oven for 30 minutes with oven door slightly open to prevent cheesecake from cracking.

15. Remove from oven and chill for 3 hours.

16. To make topping, mix together butter, walnut halves, and salt.

17. Place walnuts on a cookie sheet and bake in a preheated 350° F. oven for 4 to 5 minutes, until crisp.

18. Place on top of chilled cheesecake.

19. Serve cheesecake with a glass of vintage port wine.

Yield: One 10-inch cheesecake

· BANANA MACADAMIA CHEESECAKE ·

James R. Herringer
North Miami Beach, Florida

When you have a medley that includes banana, banana liqueur, pineapple, pineapple juice, and toasted macadamia nuts, you get a rich cheesecake with a thick, luscious glaze that will please everyone.

CRUST

½ cup macadamia nuts, toasted
2 cups cinnamon graham cracker crumbs

6 tablespoons butter, melted

FILLING

2½ pounds cream cheese, softened
2 cups superfine sugar
4 eggs
1 egg yolk
¼ teaspoon salt

½ cup crème de banana liqueur
½ cup fresh banana puree
½ cup coarsely ground toasted macadamia nuts

GLAZE

1 cup fresh pineapple puree
1 cup pineapple juice

1 cup pineapple preserves

GARNISH

whole macadamia nuts   *fresh mint leaves*

1. Preheat oven to 350° F.
2. To toast macadamia nuts, spread nuts on a cookie sheet and bake for 5 minutes or until nuts are lightly browned.
3. Increase oven temperature to 400° F.
4. To make crust, place toasted macadamia nuts and graham cracker crumbs in a processor and pulse until finely ground.
5. Combine with butter, mixing together well.
6. Press into the bottom and up the sides of a 10-inch springform pan.
7. Bake for 5 minutes, remove from oven, and set aside to cool.
8. Reduce oven temperature to 350° F.
9. To make filling, with an electric mixer set on medium speed beat cream cheese until fluffy.
10. Beat in sugar until smooth.
11. Add eggs, one at a time.
12. Add egg yolk, salt, crème de banana liqueur, and banana puree.
13. Increase mixing speed and continue to beat until batter becomes fluffy and increases in volume. The more air beaten into the batter, the lighter the texture of the finished cheesecake.
14. Fold in ground toasted macadamia nuts.
15. Wrap foil around bottom and sides of the springform pan. Pour batter into crust and place springform pan into a large roasting pan filled with water halfway up the sides of the springform pan.
16. Bake for 1 hour, or until set.

17. Remove from oven and roasting pan.

18. Increase oven temperature to 400° F.

19. To make glaze, combine pineapple puree, pineapple juice, and pineapple preserves in a heavy saucepan and heat to boiling.

20. Reduce heat and simmer until mixture becomes thick.

21. Remove from heat, let cool, and spread a thin layer evenly over top of cheesecake. Set aside extra glaze that is not used.

22. Bake for 10 minutes.

23. Remove from oven and let cool on a wire rack for 1 to 2 hours.

24. Garnish cooled cheesecake with macadamia nuts and mint leaves. Serve with extra glaze, if desired.

Yield: One 10-inch cheesecake

· WHITE CHOCOLATE AMARETTO CHEESECAKE ·

Maryann Pirog Stevens
Pasadena, California

Crunchy crust, almond flavor, and light texture are all together in one delightful and unusual white chocolate dessert.

CRUST

2½ cups almond shortbread cookie
   crumbs
½ cup almonds, finely chopped

2 ounces white chocolate, grated
½ cup butter, melted

FILLING

2 pounds cream cheese, softened
5 eggs
1 cup sugar
3 tablespoons amaretto liqueur

1 teaspoon almond extract
½ teaspoon vanilla
6 ounces white chocolate, grated

TOPPING

2 cups sour cream
¼ cup sugar

½ teaspoon almond extract

GARNISH

almond slivers

1. To make crust, mix together cookie crumbs, chopped almonds, white chocolate, and butter.
2. Pat into the bottom of a 10-inch springform pan. Set aside.
3. Preheat oven to 350° F.
4. To make filling, with an electric mixer set on medium speed, beat cream cheese until smooth.
5. Add eggs, one at a time, mixing well after each addition.
6. Add sugar, amaretto liqueur, almond extract, vanilla, and white chocolate, mixing well.
7. Pour cream cheese mixture into crust, place pan on a cookie sheet, and bake for 1 hour.
8. Remove pan from oven and set aside to cool for 10 minutes. Do not turn off oven.
9. To make topping, mix together sour cream, sugar, and almond extract.
10. Spoon on top of cheesecake, spreading evenly.
11. Return pan to oven and bake for 5 minutes.
12. Remove cheesecake from oven and let cool on a wire rack for 2 to 3 hours.
13. Refrigerate for at least 24 hours.
14. To make garnish, place almond slivers on a cookie sheet and bake at 350° F. for 4 to 6 minutes, until almonds are lightly browned.
15. Sprinkled toasted almonds over top of chilled cheesecake.

Yield: One 10-inch cheesecake

⋅ CHOCOLATE RASPBERRY TRUFFLE ⋅

Maryann Jaworski
Whitmore Lake, Michigan

Here is a divinely inspired marriage of rich chocolate raspberry and creamy cheesecake all wrapped up into one spectacular presentation.

CRUST

1½ cups finely crushed cream-filled
   chocolate sandwich cookie
   crumbs

2 tablespoons margarine, melted

FILLING

1½ pounds cream cheese, softened
1¼ cups sugar
3 eggs
1 cup sour cream
1 teaspoon vanilla

8 ounces cream cheese, softened
9 ounces semi-sweet chocolate,
   melted
½ cup seedless raspberry preserves

TOPPING

6 ounces semi-sweet chocolate

⅓ cup heavy cream

GARNISH

1 cup heavy cream, whipped   *mint leaves*
fresh raspberries

1. To make crust, combine cookie crumbs and margarine and press into the bottom of a 10-inch springform pan. Set aside.
2. Preheat oven to 325° F.
3. To make filling, with an electric mixer set on medium speed combine 1½ pounds cream cheese and sugar until well blended.
4. Add eggs, one at a time, mixing well after each addition.
5. Blend in sour cream and vanilla and then pour into prepared crust. Set aside.
6. Combine 8 ounces cream cheese and melted chocolate, mixing at medium speed with an electric mixer until well blended.
7. Add raspberry preserves, mixing together well.
8. Drop chocolate raspberry batter by tablespoonfuls onto plain cream cheese batter in pan. Do not swirl.
9. Bake for 1 hour and 25 minutes.
10. Remove from oven, loosen cake from sides of pan, and let cool on a wire rack for 1 to 2 hours before removing from pan.
11. To make topping, cook chocolate and heavy cream over low heat, stirring constantly, until chocolate has melted and mixture is smooth.
12. Remove from heat and spread over cooled cheesecake.
13. Chill for 4 to 6 hours.

14. Garnish chilled cheesecake with whipped cream, raspberries, and mint leaves. This cheesecake looks so lovely by itself that the topping and the garnish could be held aside and then placed on the cheesecake as it is cut and served.

Yield: One 10-inch cheesecake

• RANDI GULLER'S CHOCOLATE CHEESECAKE •

Randi Guller
South Orange, New Jersey

Here is a big, rich, dark chocolate cheesecake that's perfect for those who prefer their chocolate a little less sweet.

CRUST

5 tablespoons cocoa powder
5 tablespoons sugar
2 cups chopped walnuts

3½ cups graham cracker crumbs
¾ cup butter, melted

FILLING

12 ounces unsweetened chocolate
¾ cup butter
2 pounds cream cheese, softened
2 cups sour cream

2 tablespoons cornstarch
2 cups sugar
1 tablespoon vanilla
5 eggs, at room temperature

1. To make crust, mix together cocoa powder, sugar, walnuts, graham cracker crumbs, and butter.

2. Press firmly into the bottom of a greased 10½-inch springform pan. Set aside.

3. Preheat over to 375° F.

4. To make filling, melt chocolate and butter in the top of a double boiler, stirring together until smooth.

5. Remove from heat and set aside to cool.

6. With an electric mixer set on high speed, beat cream cheese and sour cream for 5 minutes.

7. Add chocolate mixture and beat for 5 more minutes.

8. Add cornstarch, sugar, and vanilla and mix for another 5 minutes. Scrape bowl while mixing.

9. Add eggs, one at a time, beating well after each addition.

10. Slowly pour filling into pan, being careful not to disturb crust.

11. Place springform pan in a large roasting pan. Fill roasting pan with enough hot water to come halfway up the sides of the springform pan.

12. Bake 1½ hours, or until cheesecake no longer shakes when pan is moved.

13. Let cool in oven for 1 hour with door open, then remove from oven and let cool on a wire rack for 1 hour at room temperature.

14. Refrigerate at least 6 hours before serving.

Yield: One 10½-inch cheesecake

No-Bake, Slightly Baked, and Cupcake Cheesecakes

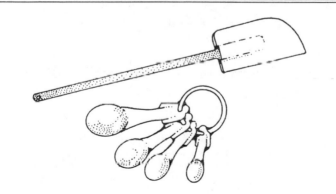

• FROZEN MOCHA FROSTCAKE •

Ruth F. Murray
Crete, Illinois

Here is a leading member of that small, elite group of truly delightful frozen homemade cheesecakes . . . and this one is extra special, with rich chocolate and coffee complemented by a crunchy cookie crust. And it's so easy to make—no-bake.

CRUST

1¼ cups chocolate wafer crumbs
¼ cup sugar

¼ cup butter or margarine, melted

FILLING

8 ounces cream cheese, softened
14 ounces sweetened condensed
    milk
⅔ cup chocolate syrup

1 tablespoon instant coffee powder
    dissolved in 1 teaspoon hot
    water
1 cup heavy cream, whipped

GARNISH

chocolate wafer crumbs

1. To make crust, combine wafer crumbs, sugar, and butter or margarine, mixing together thoroughly.

2. Pack firmly into the bottom and up the sides of a 9-inch springform pan. Set aside and chill.

3. To make filling, with an electric mixer on medium speed beat cream cheese until fluffy.

4. Add condensed milk, chocolate syrup, and dissolved coffee, mixing well.

5. Fold in whipped cream.

6. Pour filling into chilled crust. Cover and freeze for about 6 hours, or until firm.

7. Garnish with chocolate wafer crumbs.

Yield: One 9-inch cheesecake

• HOLIDAY CRANBERRY CHEESECAKE •

Sherian Erickson
Babbitt, Minnesota

A colorful cheesecake with a delightful cranberry taste that's not too sweet . . . and you don't even have to bake it.

CRUST

3/4 cup graham cracker crumbs

2 tablespoons margarine, melted

FILLING

2 cups whole unblemished
   cranberries, rinsed and
   drained
2/3 cup water
2/3 cup sugar

1 tablespoon unflavored gelatin
   dissolved in 1/4 cup cold water
8 ounces cream cheese, softened
3/4 cup ricotta cheese
1 teaspoon vanilla

GARNISH

whole cranberries

holly

1. To make crust, mix graham cracker crumbs and margarine together thoroughly and press into an 8-inch or a 9-inch pie pan. Set aside.

2. To make filling, place cranberries, water, and sugar in a saucepan, heat to boiling, and then cook at a boil for 10 minutes, stirring occasionally.

3. Remove from heat and add gelatin mixture, stirring until dissolved.

4. Add cream cheese, ricotta cheese, and vanilla, mixing until well blended. (Some of the cranberries will break up into small pieces.)

5. Pour filling into crust and refrigerate until cheesecake is firm, approximately 3 to 4 hours.

6. Garnish with whole cranberries and holly.

Yield: One 8- or 9-inch cheesecake

• BEST P'NUTTIEST CHEESECAKE •

Dorothy M. DeWyze
Palatine, Illinois

A great combination of two all-time favorites: peanut butter and cheesecake. And you don't even have to bake it.

CRUST

¾ cup chopped peanuts
1 cup graham cracker crumbs

⅓ cup butter, melted

FILLING

12 ounces cream cheese, softened
⅔ cup creamy peanut butter
14 ounces sweetened condensed
   milk

1 teaspoon vanilla
1¾ cups whipped topping
⅓ cup fresh lemon juice

GARNISH

2 tablespoons chopped peanuts

1. To make crust, combine peanuts, graham cracker crumbs, and butter.
2. Press into the bottom of a greased 9-inch springform pan.
3. Chill for 20 minutes.
4. To make filling, with an electric mixer set on medium speed beat cream cheese and peanut butter until fluffy.
5. Gradually mix in milk.
6. Fold in vanilla, whipped topping, and lemon juice.
7. Pour into chilled crust. Garnish with peanuts. Chill 2 to 3 hours, until firm.

Yield: One 9-inch cheesecake

• PEPPERMINT CANDY CREAM CAKE •

Mrs. Ruth Womac
Port Angeles, Washington

Here is an easy-to-make peppermint treat that is, of course, a delicious cheesecake . . . and when you serve it frozen, it becomes the quintessential summer delight.

CRUST

1 cup chocolate wafer crumbs

3 tablespoons margarine, melted

FILLING

1 pound cream cheese, softened
½ cup sugar
1 tablespoon unflavored gelatin
   dissolved in ¼ cup cold water
½ cup milk

¼ cup crushed peppermint candy
1 cup heavy cream, whipped
3 ounces milk chocolate, finely
   chopped

GARNISH

whipped cream

crushed peppermint candy

1. Preheat oven to 350° F.

2. To make crust, combine wafer crumbs and margarine and press into the bottom of an 8-inch springform pan.

3. Bake for 5 minutes.

4. Remove pan from oven and let cool.

5. To make filling, with an electric mixer set on medium speed beat cream cheese and sugar, mixing until well blended.

6. Gradually add dissolved gelatin, milk, and peppermint candy, blending well.

7. Chill until slightly thickened. Fold in whipped cream and chocolate.

8. Pour batter into cooled crust and chill several hours until firm. Remove rim of pan. Cheesecake can also be served frozen.

9. Garnish with whipped cream and peppermint candy just before serving.

Yield: One 8-inch cheesecake

• APRICOT NECTAR WHIP •

Mary Ann Lee
Marco Island, Florida

This cheesecake is light and airy, with a tangy lemon and apricot flavor. The crunchy "bottom line" is a shortbread cookie crust.

CRUST

1⅓ cups finely ground shortbread cookie crumbs
½ teaspoon ground ginger

3 tablespoons butter, melted and cooled

FILLING

1 cup plus 2 tablespoons apricot nectar
1 tablespoon unflavored gelatin
12 ounces cream cheese, softened
½ cup superfine sugar

1 teaspoon fresh lemon zest
1 tablespoon fresh lemon juice
1 teaspoon vanilla
1 cup heavy cream, whipped to soft peaks

TOPPING

¼ cup plus 2 tablespoons apricot
   nectar
1 tablespoon sugar

2 teaspoons cornstarch
2 teaspoons rum

GARNISH

½ cup heavy cream, whipped

1. Preheat oven to 350° F.
2. To make crust, mix together cookie crumbs and ginger.
3. Add in butter and stir until blended.
4. Press evenly into the bottom of a greased 8-inch springform pan.
5. Bake for about 5 minutes, until lightly browned.
6. Remove from oven and set aside to cool to room temperature on a wire rack.
7. To make filling, put apricot nectar in a small saucepan and sprinkle with gelatin.
8. Stirring constantly, cook over low heat until gelatin dissolves.
9. Remove from heat and set aside to cool to room temperature.
10. With an electric mixer set on medium speed, beat cream cheese, sugar, lemon zest, lemon juice, and vanilla until smooth.
11. Add nectar mixture and beat until well blended.
12. Gently but thoroughly fold in whipped cream.
13. Pour batter into crust and refrigerate uncovered for at least 3 hours, until set.

14. To make topping, mix apricot nectar, sugar, and cornstarch in a small saucepan.

15. Cook over medium heat, stirring constantly, until mixture boils.

16. Remove from heat and stir until all lumps have dissolved.

17. Stir in rum.

18. Let cool for 10 minutes, stirring frequently.

19. Spread evenly over chilled cheesecake and refrigerate for at least 30 minutes. Remove rim of pan.

20. Garnish cheesecake around edge with whipped cream piped through a pastry bag.

Yield: One 8-inch cheesecake

Think of all the different types of desserts that are served and then try to think of which one is the most popular in the United States.

It's not an easy question.

However, in the food column of the September 15, 1985, *New York Times Magazine*, noted food experts and writers Craig Claiborne and Pierre Franey described how they posed that very question to Maida Heatter, the author of many, many best-selling dessert books.

Her immediate answer: cheesecakes.

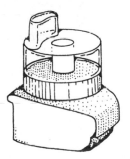

• THE BUMBLEBEE'S CHEESECAKE •

Sandra Kay Smith
Ojai, California

There's no shortage of the taste of honey, orange liqueur, and hazelnuts in this light and creamy gem.

CRUST

½ cup chopped hazelnuts
½ cup unsalted butter, melted

¼ cup honey
1½ cups graham cracker crumbs

FILLING

2 pounds cream cheese, softened
1 cup honey

½ cup orange liqueur
2 cup heavy cream, whipped stiff

GARNISH

fresh orange zest curls
fresh lemon zest curls

fresh lime zest curls

1. Preheat oven to 350° F.
2. To make crust, place chopped hazelnuts on a cookie sheet and bake for 4 to 5 minutes, until lightly toasted.

3. Remove hazelnuts from oven, let cool, and then mix with butter, honey, and graham cracker crumbs.

4. Press mixture into the bottom of a 10-inch springform pan. Set aside.

5. To make filling, with an electric mixer set on medium speed beat together cream cheese, honey, and orange liqueur.

6. Fold in whipped cream.

7. Spread filling evenly over crust and chill several hours until firm.

8. Garnish chilled cheesecake with orange, lemon, and lime zest curls.

Yield: One 10-inch cheesecake

· CUPCAKE JEWELS ·

Nina Austin
Philadelphia, Pennsylvania

Here are cute little cheesecakes—"big bite-sized"—that look like sparkling gems . . . and taste extravagant, too.

FILLING

1½ pounds cream cheese, softened
1 cup sugar
4 large eggs

½ teaspoon raspberry liqueur
½ teaspoon banana liqueur
½ teaspoon orange liqueur

TOPPING

¾ cup sour cream
¼ cup sugar
1 teaspoon vanilla

raspberry jam
strawberry jam
orange marmalade

1. Preheat oven to 300° F. Line 24 muffin tins with 24 paper muffin cups.
2. To make filling, with an electric mixer set on medium speed beat cream cheese until light and fluffy and then add sugar and eggs, one at a time. Divide batter equally into three bowls.
3. Add raspberry liqueur to ⅓ of the batter, banana liqueur to ⅓ of the batter, and orange liqueur to ⅓ of the batter.

4. Pour each ⅓ portion of the batter into 8 cupcake papers, filling each paper about ¾ full.

5. Bake for 35 minutes.

6. Remove from oven and set aside to cool for 10 minutes. The center of the cupcakes will fall slightly.

7. To make topping, mix together sour cream, sugar, and vanilla. Spoon evenly over the tops of the 24 cupcakes.

8. Place a dollop of raspberry jam on top of each raspberry liqueur cupcake, a dollop of strawberry jam on top of each banana liqueur cupcake, and a dollop of orange marmalade on top of each orange liqueur cupcake.

9. Return cupcakes to the oven and bake for 5 minutes more.

10. Remove from oven, let cool slightly, and then chill in the refrigerator for 4 to 6 hours.

Yield: 24 cupcake-sized cheesecakes

Cheesecakes from
Special Places

• PINEAPPLE COCONUT CHEESECAKE •

Queen Elizabeth 2
Cunard Line

Executive Chef Bernhard Stumpsel

COCONUT CRUST

1²/₃ cups shredded coconut
3 tablespoons sliced almonds

6 tablespoons butter, melted,
12 one-inch canned pineapple rings

LEMON CHEESE FILLING

24 ounces cream cheese
³/₄ cup granulated sugar
¹/₂ cup sour cream
5 teaspoons cornstarch
3 eggs

1 egg yolk
3 tablespoons lemon juice
3 lemon peels, grated
2 tablespoons vanilla extract

LEMON TOPPING

1 cup whipping cream
1 teaspoon sugar
1 teaspoon grated lemon peel

shredded coconut
cocoa powder

1. To make crust, stir the coconut, almonds, and melted butter together and press evenly into the bottom of a 9-inch springform pan.

2. Place the pineapple rings on top of the coconut crust.

3. To make filling, mix cream cheese, sugar, sour cream, and cornstarch together, stirring in the eggs and the egg yolk, one at a time.

4. Next add the lemon juice, lemon peels, and vanilla extract and mix well for 2 minutes.

5. Pour the mixture on the base with the pineapples and bake it for 15 minutes at 350° F.

6. Lower the temperature to 225° F. and bake for another 70 minutes, or until the center no longer looks wet.

7. Turn off the oven and cut the cake around the inside of the cake pan. Return the cake to the oven for another 60 minutes (with the heat off), then place it in the refrigerator and chill it overnight.

8. To make topping, whip up the cream, sugar, and lemon peel till stiff peaks form. Spread it over the chilled cake and sprinkle the cake with shredded coconut. Sieve the cake lightly with cocoa powder.

Yield: One 9-inch cheesecake

· PLAZA CHEESECAKE ·

The Plaza
New York, New York

Executive Chef Bruno Tison

CRUST

4 cups graham cracker crumbs
½ cup granulated sugar
pinch of salt

1 cup sweet (unsalted) butter,
   melted, warm

FILLING

3 pounds (6 8-ounce packages)
   Philadelphia Cream Cheese,
   softened to room temperature
1¾ cups granulated sugar

1 pint sour cream
7 whole fresh eggs
2 cups heavy whipping cream
⅛ cup vanilla extract

TOPPING

Fresh fruit (optional)

whipped cream (optional)

1. Preheat oven to 325° F.
2. Butter and flour two 9-inch by 3-inch round cake pans. Set aside.

3. In a medium bowl, combine graham cracker crumbs, ½ cup of sugar, and salt.

4. Add melted butter and combine. Arrange crumb mixture evenly and to a thickness of about ¼ inch in the bottom of the 2 pans.

5. Beat softened cream cheese with sugar until smooth and fluffy—scrape bowl and beaters to ensure thorough mixing.

6. Add sour cream; incorporate until smooth.

7. Add eggs one at a time on low speed. Scrape bowl and beaters between additions.

8. Add cream and vanilla, beating on low until smooth.

9. Pour mixture into 2 prepared cake pans. Place pans in water bath that comes at least halfway up sides of pans. Bake for 45 to 50 minutes, or until knife blade inserted 2 inches off center is clean when removed.

10. Remove pans from oven and allow to cool thoroughly for 5 to 6 hours in refrigerator or preferably overnight.

11. Unmold by gently warming the bottom and sides of the mold and inverting onto a large plate; tap gently to loosen from mold—invert serving platter onto bottom and turn right side up (do this carefully).

12. Serve with fresh fruit and whipped cream, if desired.

Yield: Two 9-inch cheesecakes

• CHEESECAKE •

The Lodge at Pebble Beach
Pebble Beach, California

Executive Chef Beat Giger

FILLING AND CRUST

2¼ pounds cream cheese
1½ cups sugar
7 whole eggs
5 egg yolks

1 cup half-and-half
1 teaspoon vanilla
zest of ½ lemon
2 cups graham cracker crumbs

TOPPING

1 cup sour cream
½ cup powdered sugar

raspberries and raspberry sauce
(optional, in place of sour cream
topping)

1. To make filling and crust, mix cream cheese and sugar well.
2. Add whole eggs to mixture slowly, then add egg yolks.
3. Scrape down sides of bowl and add half-and-half, vanilla, and lemon zest.
4. Grease two 9-inch springform pans and sprinkle graham cracker crumbs

on bottoms of pans. Pour batter into pans. Bake in a water bath at 350° F. for 45 minutes to 1 hour, or until firm.

5. To make topping, mix together sour cream and sugar. Spread mixture on top of cheesecake.

6. Bake for 5 minutes.

7. Note: You may also top the cheesecake with fresh raspberries and raspberry sauce in place of the sour cream topping. When using this raspberry topping, let cheesecake cool completely first.

Yield: Two 9-inch cheesecakes

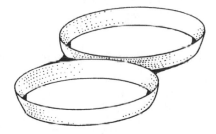

· CHEESECAKE WITH STRAWBERRY TOPPING ·

Opryland Hotel
Nashville, Tennessee

Executive Chef Richard Gerst

CRUST

5 ounces butter	1 cup plus 2 tablespoons flour
1/4 cup sugar	1 tablespoon baking powder
1/2 cup filberts	1 tablespoon cinnamon
1/2 cup cake crumbs	salt
1 egg	vanilla

FILLING

2 pounds cream cheese	5 eggs
7/8 cup sugar	juice of 1 lemon
1/4 cornstarch	dash of vanilla
9 ounces sour cream	dash of salt

TOPPING

⅔ *cup fresh crushed strawberries*   ⅜ *Grand Marnier liqueur*
¼ *cup granulated sugar*

1. Mix all crust ingredients together and press into a 9-inch springform pan.
2. Combine all filling ingredients together and pour into crust.
3. Bake at 300° F. for 45 minutes.
4. Mix together topping ingredients and spoon over top of baked cheesecake.

Yield: One 9-inch cheesecake

· CLASSIC CHEESECAKE ·

The Greenbrier
White Sulphur Springs, West Virginia

CRUST

1¼ cups graham cracker crumbs
¼ cup granulated sugar

8 tablespoons (1 stick) unsalted
  butter, melted

FILLING

3 pounds cream cheese, softened at
  room temperature
1½ cups sugar
3 tablespoons lemon juice

1 tablespoon lemon zest
1 tablespoon vanilla extract
pinch of salt
6 eggs

TOPPING

fresh fruit compote (optional)

1. Preheat oven to 375° F.
2. Mix the graham cracker crumbs, ¼ cup of sugar, and melted butter together and press into an even layer on the bottom and sides of a 10-inch springform pan. (Don't worry if the sides aren't perfectly covered.)

3. Bake in the preheated oven until slightly toasted, about 5 minutes.

4. Remove from the oven and cool. Reduce the oven temperature to 300° F.

5. With an electric mixer or a wooden spoon, cream together the softened cream cheese and sugar.

6. Add the lemon juice, lemon zest, vanilla, and salt, then add the eggs one at a time, beating well after each addition.

7. Pour the batter into the cooled crust and bake in the preheated oven until the center of the cake is no longer wobbly, about 1½ hours.

8. When the cake is cooked, turn off the oven, partially open the oven door, and let the cake cool for 2 hours before removing. (The gradual reduction in temperature will help prevent cracking.)

9. Remove the cake from the oven and cool completely at room temperature. Run a sharp knife around the inside of the springform pan to loosen the cake, then remove the ring and transfer the cake to a serving plate. Serve plain or topped with fresh fruit compote. This slightly dense but extremely creamy cake is truly a classic—and the perfect foil for a colorful fresh fruit topping.

Yield: One 10-inch cheesecake

⋅ PECAN CHEESECAKE ⋅

Williamsburg Inn
The Colonial Williamsburg Foundation
Williamsburg, Virginia

Executive Pastry Chef Marcel Walter

CRUST

2 cups graham cracker meal
½ cup finely chopped pecans

½ cup granulated sugar
4½ ounces butter, melted

FILLING

½ cup granulated sugar
½ cup light brown sugar
1½ pounds cream cheese
4 whole eggs

1 cup sour cream
⅓ cup half-and-half
1 cup toasted pecan pieces

GARNISH

12 to 14 toasted pecan halves

1. To make crust, mix all ingredients and press into buttered 10-inch cheesecake pan.

2. To make filling, cream the sugars and cream cheese for 3 minutes on medium speed with a paddle.

3. Mix in eggs, then sour cream.

4. When all is well mixed, add half-and-half.

5. Add toasted pecan pieces last.

6. Pour mixture into prepared cake tin and bake in preheated oven at 325° F. until center feels warm to the touch, approximately 45 minutes. The cake will rise slightly in the middle when done. Note: The cake pan is set and baked in about one inch of water.

7. Remove pan from oven and let cake cool. Cake can be turned out easily by warming bottom again.

8. Decorate top with pecan halves.

9. Note: Make cake two days before serving; the flavor will be much better. This cake freezes well.

Yield: One 10-inch cheesecake

· WHITE CHOCOLATE MACADAMIA CHEESECAKE ·

Four Seasons Hotel at Beverly Hills
Los Angeles, California

Executive Pastry Chef Donald Wressell

MACADAMIA GRAHAM CRUST

*½ cup toasted macadamia nuts,
    chopped fine*
¾ cup graham cracker crumbs

¼ cup brown sugar
¼ cup butter, melted

FILLING

2½ pounds cream cheese
1¼ cups sugar
6 whole eggs
½ cup sour cream
1 cup heavy cream

*2 cups chopped toasted macadamia
    nuts*
8 ounces melted white chocolate
1¼ cups Myers's rum

GARNISH

toasted macadamia nuts
white chocolate shavings

whipped cream
fresh strawberries

1. To make crust, toss all ingredients together in a bowl and press into a 10-inch springform pan. Set aside until ready to bake.

2. To make filling, with an electric mixer set on high speed cream the cream cheese and sugar together for 2 to 3 minutes.

3. Add eggs one by one, mixing thoroughly.

4. Add sour cream and mix for 30 seconds.

5. Add heavy cream and mix for 30 seconds.

6. Fold in remaining ingredients by hand until thoroughly mixed.

7. Bake in a 10-inch springform pan at 275° F. for 1 hour and 45 minutes until set. Cool.

8. Garnish with toasted macadamia nuts, white chocolate shavings, and whipped cream with fresh strawberries.

Yield: One 10-inch cheesecake

• ICEBOX CHEESECAKE •

The Hay-Adams Hotel
Washington, D.C.

Patissier Karl Unterholzner

Line two 9-inch springform pans with either baked sugar dough crust or with a thin layer of sponge cake. (Chocolate sponge cake is preferred.)

FILLING

½ cup plain yogurt
1½ pounds cream cheese
5½ ounces sugar
4 egg yolks
3½ cups lightly whipped cream
¾ cup raspberry puree (or passion fruit puree)

4 ounces chopped bittersweet chocolate
1 ounce powdered gelatin mixed into 2½ ounces cold water and placed in the top of a double boiler over boiling water to dissolve

TOPPING

whipped cream
raspberries

mint leaves

1. Cream the yogurt and cream cheese.
2. Add sugar and egg yolks.
3. Fold in whipped cream, raspberry or passion fruit puree, and chocolate.
4. Mix in dissolved gelatin.
5. Pour filling into prepared molds and let set overnight in refrigerator.
6. Unmold and decorate with rosettes of whipped cream, raspberries, and mint leaves.

Yield: Two 9-inch cheesecakes

• WHITE CHOCOLATE COINTREAU CHEESECAKE •

The Hotel Hershey
Hershey, Pennsylvania

graham cracker crumbs
3 pounds cream cheese
pinch of nutmeg
6 whole eggs
⅛ cup egg yolks
1½ pounds white chocolate

6 ounces butter
¼ cup Cointreau
¾ cup heavy cream
vanilla to taste

1. Prepare two 10-inch springform pans by greasing them and then sprinkling them with graham cracker crumbs.
2. Cream the cream cheese with nutmeg until smooth.
3. Slowly add whole eggs and egg yolks and mix until smooth.
4. Melt chocolate and butter together.
5. Add to cream cheese and egg mixture. Mix until smooth.
6. Add Cointreau.
7. Add heavy cream.
8. Add vanilla (to taste).
9. Pour batter into prepared pans. Bake in a water bath at 325° F. for 50 minutes to 1 hour.

Yield: Two 10-inch cheesecakes

• THE RITZ-CARLTON'S PUMPKIN CHEESECAKE •

The Ritz-Carlton
Boston, Massachusetts

Pastry Chef Paw Mikkelsen

¼ cup sour cream
2 pounds cream cheese, softened
¾ cup sugar
7 eggs

1 pound pumpkin
cinnamon
nutmeg

1. Add sour cream to the softened cream cheese: blend in sugar.
2. Add eggs slowly.
3. To this mixture add pumpkin, then cinnamon and nutmeg to taste.
4. Pour mixture into two 9-inch springform pans. Bake in a water bath at 325° F. for 1½ hours.
5. Note: Any flavor (other than pumpkin) may be added to the basic recipe.

Yield: Two 9-inch cheesecakes

• CHOCOLATE ESPRESSO CHEESECAKE •

El Tovar
Grand Canyon, Arizona

Pastry Chef Kathy Holman

CHOCOLATE COOKIE CRUST

1 cup chocolate cookie crumbs
2 tablespoons melted butter

1 tablespoon sugar

FILLING

8 ounces bittersweet chocolate,
    chopped
2 pounds cream cheese
1 cup sugar
1 cup sour cream

2 large eggs plus 2 egg yolks
¼ cup freshly brewed espresso
1 teaspoon vanilla extract
1 tablespoon freshly ground coffee

CHOCOLATE GANACHE

8 ounces whipping cream
6 ounces bittersweet chocolate,
    chopped

1 tablespoon instant espresso
    dissolved in 2 tablespoons water

1. To make crust, mix together all ingredients in a bowl.

2. Press into the bottom of a 9-inch springform pan. Refrigerate crust while making cheesecake.

3. To make filling, melt chocolate in the top of a double boiler and set aside to cool.

4. With an electric mixer, cream the cream cheese and sugar till light and fluffy.

5. Add sour cream and mix. Scrape down sides of bowl.

6. Add eggs and egg yolks till well mixed. Scrape down sides.

7. Add espresso, vanilla, and ground coffee. Scrape down sides.

8. Add chocolate till blended. Scrape down sides and blend mixture for a minute till well mixed.

9. Pour mixture into prepared crust, and place spring form pan in a water bath. Bake at 350° F. for 45 minutes.

10. Turn off oven and let cheesecake cool in oven for one hour before removing.

11. To make topping, bring cream to a boil on stove top.

12. Pour over chopped chocolate and let stand 1 minute. Stir to dissolve.

13. Stir espresso into chocolate mixture.

14. Let cool to room temperature. Pour onto top of cooled cheesecake.

15. Refrigerate to let set up. Cut and serve into 12 slices.

Yield: One 9-inch cheesecake

⋄ CREAM CHEESE CAKE ⋄

The Helmsley Palace
New York, New York

Executive Chef James Staiano

7½ pounds cream cheese
3 pounds sugar
2½ pounds sour cream
1 ounce lemon juice

vanilla extract, to taste
30 whole eggs
sponge cake (optional)
graham cracker crumbs

1. Preheat oven to 330° F.
2. Make sure all ingredients are at room temperature.
3. In a large mixing bowl, cream together the cream cheese and sugar until smooth. (Scrape down the sides of bowl once or twice during this step to ensure there are no lumps.)
4. Add sour cream, lemon juice, and vanilla. Mix until smooth.
5. Scrape down the bowl again and add the eggs gradually.
6. When half the eggs have been incorporated, scrape down the bowl one last time and gradually add the remainder of the eggs. Do not overmix.
7. Prepare five 8-inch cake molds by greasing the bottom and sides. A thin layer of sponge cake may be placed into the bottom of each pan and the graham cracker crumbs sprinkled around the sides of pans.
8. Bake in a water bath for 1 hour and 45 minutes to 2 hours.

Yield: Five 8-inch cheesecakes

As every student knows, ancient Greece had great thinkers, great leaders, great culture, and a pretty neat alphabet that is useful for writing scientific equations and naming college fraternities and sororities.

The ancient Greeks also had something else that was pretty good: cheesecake.

The earliest records describing cheesecake indicate that it was created on the ancient Greek island of Samos in the Aegean Sea sometime around 800 B.C.

Even Plato mentioned cheesecake in his writings, and every Greek province and city-state had its own special cheesecake recipe.

There was even a town near Thebes, northwest of Athens, that was named after cheesecake.

The lucky athletes who participated in the first Olympic games on the Isle of Delos in Greece in 776 B.C. ate cheesecakes to build up their energy.

Perhaps this tradition should be revived for such important modern-day competitions as the Super Bowl, the World Series, the New York and Boston marathons, and presidential election campaigns.

• BAILEYS IRISH CHEESECAKE •

The Breakers
Palm Beach, Florida

2¼ cups granulated sugar
1 tablespoon plus 1 teaspoon
  cornstarch
3⅔ cups cream cheese
3 whole eggs
½ cup half-and-half

1 tablespoon vanilla extract
½ cup Baileys Irish Cream
4 tablespoons semi-sweet chocolate,
  melted
1½ cups Oreo cookies
2 tablespoons unsalted butter

1. Preheat oven to 350° F.
2. In a mixer, and using the flat paddle, incorporate sugar and cornstarch.
3. Add cream cheese and blend until creamy.
4. Slowly add eggs, mixing continuously. Scrape bowl.
5. Add half-and-half in a slow stream. Scrape.
6. Add vanilla and Baileys Irish Cream to the melted semi-sweet chocolate. Stir until blended. Add these ingredients back to the cheese mixture.
7. In a food processor, pulverize the Oreo cookies.
8. Add butter to 1½ cups of Oreos.
9. Press crumbs into a greased cheesecake pan.
10. Place crust in oven at 350° F. for approximately 8 minutes.
11. When done and cool, pour cheesecake batter into crust.
12. Reduce oven temperature to 220° F. Place pan inside a fully ridged

sheetpan into the oven. Pour approximately 4 cups of water in sheet, making a water bath.

13. Bake approximately 1½ hours, making sure the water level stays constant, so as not to crack your cheesecake. When cake springs back when touched, it is done.

14. Cool completely and turn out on a cardboard round. Flip right side up with your serving plate. Refrigerate until service time.

Yield: One 9-inch cheesecake

• CHEESECAKE •

Marriott's Camelback Inn
Scottsdale, Arizona

Pastry Chef Denise French

CRUST

1 cup graham cracker crumbs

¼ cup margarine

FILLING

*18 ounces low-calorie cream
cheese*
1 cup sugar
⅔ cup Egg Beaters

*8 ounces semi-sweet chocolate,
melted*
1 teaspoon vanilla
⅔ cup low-calorie sour cream

TOPPING

1⅓ cups low-calorie sour cream
1 tablespoon plus 1 teaspoon sugar

½ teaspoon vanilla

1. To make crust, butter sides of 9-inch springform pan and sprinkle with dry graham cracker crumbs.

2. Mix graham cracker crumbs together with margarine and spread around springform pan, gently pressing down.

3. To make filling, blend cream cheese and sugar until smooth and fluffy.

4. Gradually add Egg Beaters; scrape the bowl, and beat well.

5. Blend in semi-sweet chocolate and vanilla.

6. Add sour cream and blend well.

7. Pour into prepared graham cracker crust.

8. Bake at 325° F. for approximately 40 minutes, turning pan after 20 minutes.

9. To make topping, mix together all ingredients and spread over baked cheesecake. Turn up oven temperature to 350° F. and bake for 5 minutes.

Yield: One 9-inch cheesecake

• VANILLA CHEESECAKE •

Nassau Inn at Palmer Square
Princeton, New Jersey

Executive Chef Michael LaCorte

Graham Cracker Crust

1 stick of butter
20 crumbled graham crackers

2 tablespoons sugar

Filling

3 pounds (48 ounces) cream cheese
6 whole eggs

1¾ cups sugar
1 tablespoon vanilla

1. To make crust, soften the butter in a bowl and mix in the graham crackers so that there are no lumps of butter.

2. Add the sugar and mix.

3. Pack the mixture into the bottom of a 10-inch springform pan. Set aside until ready to add filling.

4. To make filling, soften cream cheese in a mixer.

5. Add the eggs one at a time until all are blended in.

6. Add the sugar and vanilla; mix until smooth.
7. Pour into prepared graham cracker crust.
8. Bake 1 hour at 375° F. and let set in the oven to cool for 1 hour more.

Yield: One 10-inch cheesecake

• WHITE CHOCOLATE AND MACADAMIA • NUT CHEESECAKE

The Regent Beverly Wilshire
Beverly Hills, California

From the Pastry Kitchen of Chef Darrel Gilbert

CRUST

⅔ cup graham cracker crumbs
1 tablespoon granulated
   sugar

¼ cup toasted and chopped
   macadamia nuts
1½ ounces butter, melted

FILLING

1 pound cream cheese, room
   temperature
½ cup granulated sugar
3 eggs
¼ cup cream

3 ounces white chocolate, melted
3 ounces white chocolate chips
1 cup toasted and chopped
   macadamia nuts
1½ tablespoons dark rum

TOPPING

Fresh strawberries and whipped
   cream rosettes (optional)

1. Combine all crust ingredients in medium bowl.

2. Place mixture in 9-inch springform pan, pressing firmly into corners and halfway up the sides of pan. Set aside.

3. Place cream cheese and sugar in electric mixer with paddle attachment. Mix on low speed for 10 minutes, scraping sides of bowl to mix well.

4. Add eggs one at a time, mixing well after each addition.

5. Slowly add cream until well combined.

6. Fold in remaining ingredients.

7. Place mixture into prepared pan. Bake in a cold or room temperature water bath at 325° F. for 25 to 35 minutes or until toothpick inserted in middle comes out clean.

8. Allow to cool in refrigerator overnight.

9. Top with fresh strawberries and whipped cream rosettes if desired.

Yield: One 9-inch cheesecake (9 to 12 servings)

• OLD ORIGINAL BOOKBINDER'S •
FABULOUS CHEESECAKE

The Old Original Bookbinder's Restaurant
Philadelphia, Pennsylvania

butter
graham cracker crumbs
4 pounds cream cheese, room
  temperature
1 pound granulated sugar

7 large eggs
juice and grated rind of ¼ fresh
  lemon
1 teaspoon vanilla
pinch of salt

GARNISH

large fresh strawberries

apricot glaze

1. Preheat oven to 325° F.
2. Prepare a 10-inch springform pan by generously buttering and sprinkling it with graham cracker crumbs.
3. Blend cream cheese and sugar together in a large mixing bowl, beating until well combined.
4. Add eggs and continue beating until smooth and creamy.
5. Add lemon juice and rind, vanilla, and salt; beat until well combined.
6. Pour mixture into prepared springform pan and place into a pan of hot water in the preheated oven.

7. Bake for 1½ hours or longer if necessary. Cake should be firm around the edges and soft in the center.

8. Remove from oven; cool cheesecake in the pan.

9. Let cake stand in the refrigerator overnight before removing from the pan.

10. Garnish cheesecake with large fresh strawberries; coat the berries with an apricot glaze. Fresh California Driscoll strawberries are recommended.

Yield: One 10-inch cheesecake

Index